Seasoned in the South

Recipes Full Of Hospitality

by

Susanne Gabriel Arthur

McClanahan
Publishing House

International Standard Book Number 0-913383 86-4
Library of Congress Card Catalog Number 2002103890

Cover design, illustrations and book layout by James Asher Graphics
Cover illustration by James Asher
Back cover photo by Smith's Studio

Manufactured in the United States of America

All book order correspondence should be addressed to:

McClanahan Publishing House, Inc.
P. O. Box 100
Kuttawa, KY 42055

1-800-544-6959

www.kybooks.com
books@kybooks.com

*To my husband Bill with whom I've been cookin' for 36 years,
who has filled my seasons of life with two children, Amy and David,
and countless people and adventures.*

Introduction

Welcome to our home, y'all. Come in, pull up a chair, lean back and enjoy some of the recipes and vignettes of places I've spent the seasons of my life. Born in the South, about 50 miles south of the Mason-Dixon Line, that is, we currently live in Georgia, land of peaches, pecans, peanuts and Vidalia onions to name a few!

My Pennsylvania-born husband Bill is an ordained Presbyterian pastor, and together we've served pastorates for the last 36 years in Clarksburg, WV, Clairton, near Pittsburgh, PA, Richmond, VA, Columbia, SC, Auburn, AL, Harrisburg, PA, and now Atlanta.

We've been abundantly blessed by an ever-widening circle of friends who have showered us with love and shared with us meals, personal stories and adventures. Whether 100 people for a party or 2 for dinner, our greatest delight always is sharing with them our home, especially around the dining room table. I tell everyone that while I know nothing material goes with me to eternity, the last piece of furniture I will be sad to part with is our dining room table, around which has sat family now gone forever, our children and their friends while growing up, our new family generation, and countless friends – all making memories together.

Maybe these stories will rekindle in you similar feelings, or "smells of home", or stories of those who shared themselves with you around a table somewhere. Life is an ongoing journal and has its own seasons.

Y'all come back to see us, hear?

Table of Contents

Punches, Munchies & More 7
Breakfast & Brunch 21
Soups, Salads & Sandwiches 37
Side Items 59
Entrées 81
Breads 111
Sweet Thangs 119
After Thoughts 153

Punches, Munchies & More

Cherry

Jump-Start Juice

One frozen peeled banana
1 cup orange juice
2 to 3 frozen strawberries, optional

While visiting friends, Bob and Jean Talmage, in Auburn, parents of 6 children and entertainers of scores of friends and groups, she served this refreshing, nutritious, power-punch breakfast drink. I have since served it to house guests and my P.E.O. sorority Bed & Breakfast guests and in the Summer especially, I fix it for myself on the way out the door to work.

About 10 to 15 minutes before serving, place frozen fruit in blender and add juice. Whir to liquefy. Serves 2. Make it "classy" by serving in stemmed glasses.

What do you do with overripe bananas? Just peel and wrap individually in plastic wrap, place in freezer bag and freeze.

Icy Mocha Coffee

¼ cup instant coffee granules
½ cup sugar
2 tablespoons vanilla
½ cup boiling water
6 cups milk
¼ to ½ cup crème de cocoa

Mix together first 4 ingredients. Let cool. Add milk and crème de cocoa. Serve over ice. Makes 6½ to 7 cups. This beverage keeps in refrigerator for 3 or 4 days.

This is a fairly new recipe acquisition from a long-time childhood friend, Linda Bush Funk. We participated in each other's weddings in the mid-1960's but with career moves and family responsibilities, our lives went in different directions. Then 28 years later while living in Harrisburg, I picked up the phone and called Linda in nearby York. I gave her some I.D. puzzle pieces, after the fourth piece, she squealed, "Susanne! Where are you?" We rekindled our friendship that now includes our husbands, Bill and J.G., and have been inseparable since that telephone reunion. How wonderful that a friendship dormant for so long can flourish so profusely today.

Southern Muggy Day Pineapple Slush

Our friendship with Bob and Mary Ann Brearley has been intertwined since Richmond days. Mary Ann loves to cook and somehow gets all the duties accomplished as an active and caring pastor's wife, elementary school music teacher, attentive and nurturing mother of three, and abiding friend to scores of folks. We are always renewed, refreshed and refilled with love when we hear from these "extended family members."

One 20-ounce can crushed pineapple, undrained
⅓ to ½ cup sugar
2 to 3 bananas, mashed with fork
One 6-ounce can orange juice, diluted with
3 cans water
One 2-liter bottle lemon-lime soda
1 to 2 lemons, juiced

Mix all ingredients together and pour in 6 to 8 ounce plastic cups or pewter Jefferson cups, filling two-thirds of container. Freeze. Thaw about 1 hour before serving. Use fresh mint as a garnish. Quite refreshing on a hot Southern afternoon!

Note: Number of servings vary with size of cup used, size of lemons and bananas, and amount of slush in each cup.

One of Georgia's Nuts
The Pecan

Orange Pecans:

Chick Scarsbrook made these orange pecans for the Arthurs every Christmas we lived in Auburn.

1 ½ cups sugar
⅓ cup orange juice
3 ½ to 4 cups pecan halves

Combine sugar and juice; cook to soft ball.* Add pecan halves, coating thoroughly. With cooking oil, spray a cookie sheet. Pour nuts on sheet and bake at 350° about 20 minutes or until brown. Keeps well stored in airtight containers.

*Soft ball is when a drop of hot liquefied sugar forms a pliable ball when dropped in small container of cold water.

Spicy Pecans:

1 egg white, beaten stiffly
4 cups pecan halves
1 cup sugar
½ teaspoon salt
1 teaspoon cinnamon
½ teaspoon curry
Butter for greasing cookie sheet

In bowl whip egg white; stir in pecans, coating well. In separate bowl combine sugar, salt, cinnamon and curry. Mix well. Grease cookie sheet with butter. Spread pecans evenly on sheet and sprinkle liberally with dry ingredients. Bake at 275° for 35 minutes or until brown.Store in airtight container.

*H*ere's a life-saver when the schedule is hectic! While we appreciate items like this that are quick and simple, it is always a delight to experience the hospitality of others who go "the extra mile" and really put themselves out in preparing something very special. To me, real hospitality always involves a degree of investment of oneself. As more of us gravitate to "quick fixes," we can appreciate people who spend preparation time in the kitchen.

Always Ready Appetizers

1 loaf thin-sliced white bread
½ pound extra sharp cheddar cheese
6 to 8 slices bacon, fried and drained
4.5 ounces slivered almonds, untoasted
1 medium onion, coarsely chopped
1 cup mayonnaise
Salt and pepper

Remove crusts from bread. Set aside. Place next 4 ingredients in food processor; whir until well blended. Transfer mixture to a bowl and add mayonnaise and salt and pepper. Blend thoroughly. Spread on bread and cut each slice in 4 strips. Place on cookie sheet and bake at 400° for 10 minutes. To freeze: Put unwrapped strips on cookie sheets and freeze; then store in sealed plastic bag. Before serving, remove from freezer, place appetizers on cookie sheet and bake at 400° for 10 minutes.

Amaretto Cheese

8-ounces soft cream cheese
¼ cup Amaretto
2 tablespoons butter
One 2.25-ounce package sliced almonds
1 cup of pineapple juice or 7-Up

Place cream cheese in a bowl; stir in Amaretto; blend thoroughly. Transfer to flat serving dish. In skillet, melt butter and sauté almonds until golden brown. Cover cream cheese mixture with almonds. Serve with unpeeled apple wedges dipped in pineapple juice or 7-Up.

Tip: For the holidays, I alternate red and green apple wedges. At other times, I add color by using a variety of apples — Red Delicious, Golden Delicious, Granny Smith.

Food presentation should have different colors and textures just as you use in decorating a home or choosing personal attire. Even if your lifestyle does not include entertaining, whether they be houseguests or dinner guests, do it for yourself! Also by using variety, nutrition and fiber are more properly balanced.

Crescent Moon Baked Brie

Absolutely divine —
and a bonus from a church
young adult Gourmet Group
in Columbia where Kathy
James served Baked Brie.
Your friends will crown you
"Gourmet Queen" after they
eat this appetizer.

Cooking oil spray
3 packages crescent rolls, divided in half
One 2.2-pound or less wheel of brie cheese, cut in
1-inch cubes
1 stick butter
One 2.25-ounce package sliced almonds, toasted
One 10- to 12-ounce jar apricot preserves
2 tablespoons butter, melted
3 tablespoons brown sugar

Place foil on cookie sheet and spray with cooking oil spray.
Roll out 1½ cans crescent rolls, overlapping them so they
make a circle. Press edges together securely. Make a pyramid
of cheese in center of the "bottom crust." Cut slivers of butter and put on cheese. Sprinkle one-half of the almonds on
top. Pour apricot preserves over all in center and then sprinkle remaining almonds. Roll out the other 1½ cans crescent
rolls and place on top of pyramid. Cut 3 or 4 tiny slits in the
"top crust" for steam to escape. Securely pinch together the
edges of both crusts. Dab top crust with melted butter.
Sprinkle with brown sugar. Bake at 350° for 30 minutes or
until golden brown. Remove from oven and let rest for a
while. Serve with bland crackers.

Deluxe Beef & Pecan Spread

1 tablespoon butter
¼ to ½ cup chopped pecans
One 8-ounce block cream cheese
2 tablespoons milk
½ cup sour cream
One 2.25-ounce jar dried beef, finely chopped
¼ cup chopped green pepper
2 tablespoons dried onion flakes
¼ teaspoon pepper
¼ teaspoon garlic salt
Butter, softened

For over 20 years, each time we ate at Dottie and Bill Yingling's home in Pennsylvania, I'd leave with a terrific recipe. Not only an astute, successful businesswoman who's dedicated to improving other's lives, locally and globally, she cooks too!

In small skillet melt butter and sauté pecans. Set aside. In bowl cream together cream cheese and milk; stir in sour cream, dried beef, green pepper, onion flakes, pepper and garlic salt. Grease slightly with butter one 8-inch glass pie pan. Pour ingredients into pie pan. Top with sautéed chopped pecans. Bake in 350° oven for 20 minutes. Serve hot with crackers. This appetizer can be made ahead of time and reheated.

Mexican Roll-Ups

12 ounces cream cheese
One 4.5-ounce can chopped chilies, drained
One 2.25-ounce can chopped ripe olives, drained
½ medium onion, finely minced
½ teaspoon chili powder
6 large flour tortillas
Peach salsa or regular salsa

Mix together first 5 ingredients. Divide evenly on tortillas. Spread to edge of tortillas and roll up. Store in plastic bag - they should fit snugly to keep from unrolling - and refrigerate. When ready to serve, remove from bag and slice into 1-inch pieces. Serve with salsa.

ynn and Bill Merrill were colleagues in the Development Office of the Presbyterian Homes of Georgia. Lynn is somewhat a clone of Superwoman with giving leadership to Atlanta's Habitat for Humanity and the homeless Children's Shelter at North Avenue Presbyterian Church, raising funds to care for senior adults, and to the Session or committees at Trinity Presbyterian Church. Try these Roll-Ups, and you'll find she's not bad in the kitchen either!

Pretend-to-be-Rich & Famous Appetizer

One 13¾-ounce can quartered artichokes
6 ounces soft cream cheese
1 teaspoon lemon juice
½ teaspoon grated onion
2 tablespoons mayonnaise
One 2-ounce jar caviar
Zest from 1 lemon

Like many folks, I was wary of caviar - now I'm hooked! That first taste of Ada Folmar's Caviar appetizer in Auburn has lead to compliments galore when I serve it. Red caviar makes a bright, cheery, well-received appetizer at Christmastime. You will find a zester a utensil worth having in your kitchen. It will save lots of knuckles lost in grating!

Check to make sure artichokes are not in a marinade. Drain artichokes and squeeze to get as dry as possible. Put in food processor and whir until completely mashed. On a serving dish make a mound of the processed artichokes. In small bowl combine next 4 ingredients. "Ice" the artichoke mound with this mixture. Refrigerate. At serving time, spoon caviar over top of "icing" and add lemon zest. Serve with Melba toast, plain pita bread chips, plain or sesame bagel chips.

Sure Winner Dip

Our son-in-law Chip enjoys cooking and "tweaks" almost every recipe he tries. It's quite a diversion from his occupation as an electrical engineer, but I guess both areas involve equations and trial-and-error methods.

One 1-pound package mild or hot sausage, cooked and drained
One 10-ounce can diced tomatoes with chilies
One 8-ounce block cream cheese, softened
One 8-ounce container sour cream, optional
Tortilla chips

In skillet break sausage into small pieces and cook 'till done. With slotted spoon transfer to sauce pan and add the tomatoes with chilies and softened cream cheese. Stir in sour cream. Stir 'till mixture is well blended and thoroughly heated. Place in serving dish for scooping with tortilla chips.

Vidalia Onion Dip

1 ½ cups hand chopped Vidalia or
Sweet Texas onions
1 ½ cups shredded Swiss cheese
1 cup mayonnaise, regular or lite only
1 teaspoon sugar
Cooking spray

Mix all ingredients together. Coat one 8-inch glass pie plate. Bake at 350° for 30 minutes. Remove from oven. Lay a paper towel on top of onion mixture and gently pat to absorb any grease. Remove paper towel and sprinkle with paprika. Best served on buttery round crackers.

Tip: Hand chop the onions - food processing makes them too watery.

Fireside Hanover Pretzels

Another active and caring Eastminster Church member in Marietta and veteran Delta Airlines flight attendant, Judy Struk, passed along this recipe she received aboard one of her flights.

One 13.5-ounce box Snyder's
Hanover-Style Pretzels
1 stick butter
1 cup vegetable or canola oil
One envelope onion soup mix

Break pretzels into bite-size pieces. Melt butter; add oil and onion soup mix. Add pretzel pieces and stir until all pieces are well coated. Spread pretzels evenly onto a cookie sheet and bake in a 250° oven for 1½ hours or until the soup mixture has been absorbed. Let cool and enjoy!

Breakfast & Brunch

Dogwood

Bravo Breakfast

Brad West wears many hats and enjoys using his cooking talents rustlin' up breakfast for the men's group at Eastminster Presbyterian Church in Marietta. My husband, Bill, stood in utter amazement at Brad's effortless, unflappable ability to fix Eggs Benedict by the dozens or stacks of these tortilla treats.

3 eggs
Vegetable oil
¼ cup chopped green peppers
¼ cup chopped onions
2 tablespoons chopped fresh mushrooms
2 small flour tortillas
Soft butter for spreading and buttering griddle
¾ cup mixture of shredded Monterey Jack and
Cheddar cheeses
Guacamole
Sour cream
Salsa

In skillet scramble eggs, scoop in a bowl, and set aside. Clean and add oil to sauté vegetables. Set aside. Heat a griddle or large cast iron skillet to medium temperature and butter generously. Butter one tortilla and place buttered side down on griddle. Top with layer of scrambled eggs, then layer of vegetables. Top with cheeses and second tortilla. Spread butter on top of tortilla. As soon as cheeses melt, carefully flip stack over and heat until second tortilla is brown. Cut in half or wedges and serve with desired toppings of guacamole, sour cream, or salsa. Serves 1 or 2.

Variations: Fry 2 strips of bacon, drain and crumble, add to scrambled eggs and/or add 1 tablespoon taco seasoning mix while sautéing vegetables.

All-Seasons French Toast

Four slices French, Italian or Challah bread,
preferably stale
1 egg, beaten with fork
¼ teaspoon vanilla extract
1½ cups milk
Vegetable oil or butter
One 3-ounce box instant French vanilla pudding
Fresh grated whole nutmeg to taste
Fresh fruit of choice

Bill enjoyed this new version of French toast served by a long-time friend and fellow pastor's wife, Mary Ann Brearley at Montreat, North Carolina, in July 2001. Since then, I've served it to delighted house-guests.

Cut bread into 1-inch slices. Mix together egg, vanilla and milk. Dip bread in egg mixture until almost saturated. Heat griddle or iron skillet. Grease with oil or butter and add bread slices. Brown on both sides and the center should be cooked as well. While slices of bread are browning, make instant pudding as directed on package. When French toast is ready, transfer to platter or plate; add a dollop of the pudding and top with fruit.

Tip: If serving several folks, make French toast and keep warm on cookie sheet in 200° oven, then top with pudding and fruit at serving time.

Suggestions: In the summertime, add fresh blueberries, peaches, raspberries, blackberries, strawberries, singly or any combination; in the wintertime, bananas are delightful with a sprinkle of cinnamon. Serve with Canadian bacon, crisp bacon slices or cooked sausage links.

Early Marriage Goldenrod Eggs

6 hard-boiled eggs
2 tablespoons butter
2 tablespoons all-purpose flour
1 ½ cups milk
4 English muffins, split
Capers, drained, optional

This recipe is also easy for a crowd. Increase proportionately. "Gourmet it up" by adding a few capers on top of sprinkled egg yolks. Given to me when I was first married by Dora Faye Smith, I've used it countless times, always reliving times with her.

Peel hard-boiled eggs; cut in half and remove yolks. Press yolks through a sieve so they can be sprinkled; set aside. In saucepan melt butter and whisk or stir in flour until smooth; gradually add milk, stirring constantly making a medium white sauce. Remove from stove. Chop egg whites into sauce. Cover and keep hot. Toast muffin halves and pour mixture on each half. Sprinkle with egg yolks. Serve with a thin slice of ham and some fruit for a special eye-appealing and tasty breakfast. Serves 4.

Eggs in Herb Tomato Sauce

8 tablespoons olive oil
2 cloves garlic, halved
1 onion, minced
30 ounces tomato sauce
1 teaspoon dried thyme
1 teaspoon dried sweet basil
2 teaspoons dried parsley
Salt and pepper
8 eggs
French bread

First Presbyterian Church members in Auburn, Clarence and Chick Scarsbrook, "adopted" us as family and would on a whim call us to come share a meal with them or take home their garden bounty. One morning this egg recipe was our breakfast. Both are in the Winter season of their lives now but oh, how they've filled all their seasons together by sharing and caring for family and friends and their dear church and for sharing intellect and experiences, expanding the minds of those among them. May their kind increase!

Heat oil in saucepan that has a tight-fitting lid. Split garlic cloves lengthwise and run a toothpick in each piece. Brown garlic slowing in oil. Add minced onion and cook slowly 10 minutes or until golden. Add tomato sauce and all seasonings and herbs. Cook 15 minutes, stirring often. When done, remove garlic and toothpicks and discard. Break eggs into barely boiling sauce, spacing evenly in saucepan. Spoon sauce over them, cover and cook slowly for 20 minutes or until eggs are cooked through. Toast thinly sliced French bread in oven. Remove and place on plate. Carefully, with large spoon, lift eggs from sauce and place on toast. Spoon additional sauce over the eggs. Serves 4 to 8.

Professor Pam Boyd at Auburn University shared this quick and delicious recipe with me. Although the coconut is what makes it "ambrosia," some folks do not like coconut. For these non-coconut eaters, separate the recipe and adjust quantity of coconut accordingly.

Ambrosia of The Gods

3 Golden Delicious apples
One 6-ounce can frozen orange juice, thawed
One 6-ounce can water
One 6-ounce package frozen coconut
One 8-ounce can crushed pineapple, undrained
Maraschino cherries with stem

Core apples but do not peel; grate by hand or in food processor. In non-metallic container, mix apples together with orange juice concentrate, water, coconut and pineapple. Let stand overnight in refrigerator. Serve in dessert dishes, wine glasses or other glass or crystal stemware for breakfast, brunch or as a refreshing dessert. Garnish with Maraschino cherries.

Either through reading or talking with others, the phrase "grazing" for brunches or parties is when you do not sit down but hold a plate, "grazing" with a bite of this and a bite of that. It's a great way to taste everything, zero in on what you really find tasty, and no one knows how much quantity you consume!! Jackie Lunsford who lived in Verona, Italy, introduced me to this combination of melon and Prosciutto ham where it's a favorite Summer appetizer.

Melon Wrap

For "grazing" affairs, cut ripe honeydew or cantaloupe melon in bite-size chunks and wrap with Prosciutto ham; secure with toothpick.

For a sit-down breakfast or brunch or as an appetizer, cut honeydew or cantaloupe melon in 12 slivers. Carefully remove rind; set aside. On round serving platter, arrange rind slivers to radiate from center. Place a melon sliver on the rind, sprinkle lightly with fresh ground black pepper and fold one slice Prosciutto ham on each sliver. For more color and taste, I use both melons on the same platter.

Maple Bacon Oven Pancake

2 eggs
¼ cup maple syrup
1 tablespoon sugar
¾ cup milk
1½ cups biscuit mix
2 cups shredded Cheddar cheese, divided
12 slices bacon, cooked crisp and crumbled

The Maple Bacon Oven Pancake was first served at a meeting of P.E.O., a philanthropic sorority for the higher education of women. This pancake has become a frequent "repeater" for our family and house-guests. As a financial contribution to the sorority's educational projects, the P.E.O. Bed & Breakfast locus is our home. This pancake is always a favorite breakfast items of the guests.

In a mixing bowl beat together eggs, maple syrup, sugar, milk, biscuit mix and ½ cup cheese. Pour batter into greased and floured 9 x 13-inch pan and bake in 425° oven for 10 to 15 minutes or until toothpick comes out clean. Sprinkle with remaining 1½ cups cheese and top with crumbled bacon. Return to oven 1 minute to melt cheese. Serve with syrup.

Variations: Add 1 cup fresh blueberries to pan before pouring batter. The batter will barely cover the berries but that is all right. Or, cooked, crumbled sausage may be used instead of bacon.

Anytime Cheesy Egg Bake

Columbia friend, Paige Parsons, says her family has used this casserole for years from breakfast to light supper meals.

Two 10¾-ounce cans cream of chicken soup
1 cup milk
4 teaspoons minced onion
1 teaspoon prepared yellow mustard
One 8-ounce package shredded Swiss cheese
12 eggs
12 slices white bread, cut in half diagonally

In saucepan or suitable dish for microwave, mix together soup, milk, onion and mustard. Heat until smooth. Remove from heat and stir in Swiss cheese, stirring until cheese melts. Pour 1 cup of this sauce in a 9 x 13-inch flat casserole and using the back of a large spoon, make 12 wells for the eggs. Break 1 egg into each well. If they run together, don't worry. Spoon remaining sauce over eggs. Stand triangles of bread around inside of dish edge, overlapping slightly. Bake in 350° oven for 20 minutes. Do not overcook. Eggs may not look done, but they will be. Serves 12. This recipe is an easy one to divide in half for 6 servings, using a smaller casserole.

Indoor Grill Breakfast Apple Tortilla

See how folks like Paige Parsons, with a busy schedule save time?

1 small crisp apple
One 6-inch flour tortilla
1 slice Swiss cheese
Cinnamon
Sugar or sugar substitute
Cooking oil spray

Preheat indoor grill 5 minutes. Slice unpeeled apple as thinly as possible; set aside. On flour tortilla, place cheese slice and arrange apple slices in an overlapping circle. Sprinkle apple slices with cinnamon and sugar or sugar substitute. Spray top of stack with cooking oil spray. Lower upper grill lid and grill on preheated grill about 3 minutes until golden on the bottom, cheese is melted and apples are slightly cooked. Remove from grill and serve. Be careful — it will be hot! Single serving.

Pap Pap's Pancakes

2 eggs
⅓ cup vegetable oil
3 cups buttermilk
1 cup all-purpose flour
¼ cup cornmeal
¾ cup whole wheat flour
1 teaspoon baking soda
1 tablespoon wheat germ
1 teaspoon salt
3 teaspoons baking powder
Sprinkle of sugar

Bill's father, Pap Pap as Amy and David called him, used to make stacks of these pancakes for our son David from the time David was highchair age until he was 6 years old. David never knew that Pap Pap actually used buttermilk in these pancakes!

Beat with mixer eggs, oil, buttermilk and flour. In separate bowl combine cornmeal and whole wheat flour; stir to mix. Add remaining ingredients. Add to first mixture and beat with mixer until thoroughly mixed. Grease griddle with bacon and heat until drops of water dance, then pour batter. Flip sides when ready. Cover and store the leftover batter in refrigerator for a few days. The batter will be thick but may be thinned with additional buttermilk or water. Pap Pap used to make waffles with this batter, omitting the sugar.

Popular Cheese & Eggs with a Twist

8 slices white bread, cubed

1 ½ cups grated sharp Cheddar cheese

6 eggs

2 cups milk

Dash of pepper

¼ teaspoon salt

½ teaspoon dry mustard

1 pound bacon or sausage or cooked, shaved ham

⅓ cup chopped onion, optional

⅓ cup chopped green pepper, optional

One 10 ¾-ounce can cream of mushroom soup

½ cup milk

As the mother of a big family, as the hostess for dinner parties, and as a frequent large-crowd volunteer cook at Eastminster Presbyterian Church in Stone Mountain, Lynne Scott has some fabulous recipes. Her recipe with the additional topping elevates this everyday casserole to the gourmet classification!! Try it for supper some evening.

Put bread cubes in 9 x 13-inch flat glass casserole. Top with Cheddar cheese. In a bowl beat next 5 ingredients. Pour on top of cheese. In skillet or microwave, cook and crumble bacon or sausage, reserving grease to sauté onions and peppers, if desired. Cover with foil and refrigerate overnight. When ready to bake, mix together the soup and milk. Pour over top and bake uncovered at 325° for 1 to 1 ½ hours. Serves 8 to 10.

Meal-in-One Egg Casserole

4 tablespoons margarine
½ pound sliced dried beef in jars, chopped
3 slices bacon, diced and slightly cooked
One 6-ounce jar sliced mushrooms, drained
½ cup all-purpose flour
1 quart milk
Pepper
1 cup evaporated milk
16 eggs
½ teaspoon salt
6 additional tablespoons margarine

A bridge group that had met for years, most of who were members of Shandon Church in Columbia and became our friends, feted Chip and Amy with a lovely pre-wedding brunch in 1992 at the home of Gene and Susan Rogers. Another hostess in the group, Georgene Tapp's casserole recipe went home in my pocketbook and was served at a brunch following yet another milestone event, the baptism of our granddaughter, Mary Elizabeth, in 1998.

In large skillet melt 4 tablespoons margarine; sauté chopped dried beef, bacon and mushrooms. Add flour and stir thoroughly. Add milk and a slight amount of pepper. Stir until thickened and set aside. In a bowl whip together evaporated milk, eggs and salt. In a second large skillet melt 6 tablespoons margarine and add egg mixture. Cook to a very soft scramble (the eggs will cook more in the oven). In a buttered 3-quart flat casserole, place one-third beef mixture; layer with one-half scrambled eggs; repeat; ending with last third beef mixture. Cover securely and refrigerate overnight. Remove cover and bake at 300° for 1 hour.

Frosty Morn Sausage Coffee Cake

Joanne Clark, a gifted musician and artist friend, shared this recipe with me in 1986 during our days together in Columbia.

1 pound sausage

½ cup chopped onion

¼ cup Parmesan cheese

½ cup grated Swiss cheese

1 egg, beaten

¼ teaspoon Tabasco

1½ teaspoons salt

2 tablespoons fresh parsley

2 cups biscuit mix

¾ cup milk

¼ cup mayonnaise

1 egg yolk

1 tablespoon water

Brown sausage and onion; drain. Add next 6 ingredients. In a separate bowl make batter of biscuit mix, ¾ cup milk and mayonnaise. Grease an 11 x 7 x 2-inch pan. Pour in and spread one-half of batter. Pour in sausage mixture, then spread remaining batter on top. Mix egg yolk with water and brush on top. Bake at 400° for 25 to 30 minutes or until cake leaves sides of pan. Cool 5 minutes before cutting into 3-inch squares.

Skillet Almond Coffee Cake

This recipe was shared with me by my office mate, Mary Ann Cox, when I worked at the Southern Territorial Headquarters of The Salvation Army here in Atlanta.

¾ cup real butter, melted
1½ cups sugar
2 eggs
1½ cups all-purpose flour
½ teaspoon salt
1 teaspoon almond flavoring
Spray cooking oil
One 2.25-ounce package slivered almonds, toasted
Aerosol can whipping cream
4 Maraschino cherries, halved

Cream butter and sugar until smooth. Add eggs, one at a time, beating well after each addition. Add flour, salt and almond flavoring to creamed mixture; mix well. Line oven-proof 10-inch cast iron skillet with aluminum foil, extending foil above edge. Spray with cooking oil. Pour batter into skillet. Sprinkle with almonds, reserving a few for garnish. Bake at 350° for 30 to 40 minutes. Cool in skillet. Lift out foil. Gently tear foil away from cake and place on serving plate or cake stand. Cut into wedges and serve with a dollop of whipping cream, maraschino cherries and a few almond slivers. It's even great just plain.

Note: Only an iron skillet should be used for even temperature baking surface.

Hoppin' Red Bunny

2 tablespoons all-purpose flour
½ cup milk
1 cup tomato juice
3 eggs, lightly beaten
2 teaspoons yellow mustard
⅛ to ¼ teaspoon cayenne pepper
Salt and pepper to taste
2 cups Longhorn cheese, grated

Place flour in jar or shaker; add milk and shake vigorously 'till thoroughly mixed and pour into heavy saucepan. Stir in tomato juice, eggs, mustard, cayenne pepper, salt and pepper. Add cheese. Stir constantly and cook until thick. Adjust mustard, salt and peppers to taste. It should have a rich, cheese flavor with a "little kick." Serve over toasted white bread for a brunch or light lunch. It's "quick as a bunny" to fix!

In the early 1940's, my parents made life-long friends with Wade and Wanda Coffindaffer. My "adopted sister" was their daughter, Connie Sue. I cannot remember life without those three people, and Wanda is now dubbed "My Other Mother," as is my dear mother-in-law, Mary. When I think of childhood fun times, especially eating Red Bunny for breakfast or supper, being with the Coffindaffers ranks high.

Hearty Hash Brown Omelet

4 slices bacon
2 cups frozen hash browns, cooked
¼ cup chopped onion
¼ cup chopped green pepper
One 4.5-ounce can green chilies, optional
4 eggs
¼ cup milk
Salt and pepper to taste
4 thick slices Velveeta

Whether it's playing bridge or tennis, lending a helping hand, dropping a note to someone, rescuing an animal, serving as a Ruling Elder at Shandon Presbyterian Church in Columbia, or organizing a fun event, Jean Weldon gets it all done. We were often hosted by the Weldons and enjoyed this omelet one morning for breakfast. She and Hugh were some of the first ones who made Columbia become home for the Arthurs.

In 10 to 12-inch skillet fry bacon 'till crisp, reserving grease. Drain and crumble bacon. Pour off some grease. In bowl mix hash browns, onion, green pepper and chilies. Pat into skillet and cook over low heat until underside is crisp and brown. With fork, blend eggs with milk, salt and pepper. Pour over hash brown mixture. Top with bacon and cheese pieces. Cover. Cook over low heat for 10 minutes. Loosen and serve in wedges. All you need is some fruit, juice and toast. This would also make a good supper meal.

Soups, Salads & Sandwiches

Peony

 Corn Soup
(Sopa de Elote San Miguel)

The whole kernel corn is a personal addition to this soup recipe of Betje Klier, Ph.D., a former professor of Foreign Language Education at Auburn University. A Texan by birth, Dr. Klier brought all sorts of new information about Texas, Louisiana, Mexico and France and history in general to my knowledge bank.

4 cups frozen corn
1 cup water
¼ cup butter
3½ cups milk
One 11-ounce can whole kernel corn, drained
Monterey Jack cheese, grated
One 4.5-ounce canned green chilies, drained
Tortilla chips, broken
Salt and pepper

Place corn and water in blender; whir at high speed to make smooth purée. Melt butter in large saucepan, stirring carefully and making sure it does not burn. Add corn purée and cook over medium heat 5 minutes. Slowly add milk and bring mixture to a boil. Lower heat and let simmer 15 minutes, or until thickened, stirring frequently. Add whole kernel corn for texture. Place into soup bowls and add generous portions of Monterey Jack cheese and diced green chilies. Sprinkle top with tortilla chips. Salt and pepper to taste. Serves 4.

Taco Soup

2 pounds ground beef
1 large onion, chopped
Three 16-ounce cans refried beans
One 16-ounce can whole corn, including liquid
One 16-ounce can diced tomatoes, including liquid
One 15-ounce can tomato sauce
1½ cups water
One 4.5-ounce can green chopped chilies,
with liquid
One 1.25-ounce packet taco seasoning
1 package dry ranch dressing

Toppings:

Cheddar and/or Monterey Jack cheese
Sour cream

This is a hearty, tasty duo my Columbia friend, Jackie Lunsford, served us, and our family and guests always say "yummm."

In large pot brown ground beef and onion; drain off excess fat. Add remaining ingredients. Simmer about 30 minutes, stirring frequently as the refried beans sink to the bottom of the pan and tend to stick or burn. Serve topped with grated Cheddar and/or Monterey Jack cheese and a dollop of sour cream. Delicious with Broccoli or Spinach Cornbread — see Bread section — and a tossed green salad. Serves 8.

Tortellini and Leek Soup

Another soup recipe from Jackie!

2½ cups milk
1 cup water
One envelope leek onion soup mix
One 1.8-ounce plastic container prepared tortellini

In saucepan place milk and water; stir soup mix into liquids. Bring almost to boil over medium high heat; lower heat to low setting, partially cover saucepan and simmer 10 minutes. Add tortellini and continue simmering until tortellini is heated through. If necessary, add more milk or water to make desired soup consistency. Serve with Italian bread and tossed salad. Serves 3 to 4.

President's Soup

1 pound large, dry lima beans
1 small bunch carrots
1 small bunch celery
2 to 3 onions
2 to 3 white potatoes
2 sticks real butter
1 cup Minute rice
One 6-ounce can tomato paste
1 teaspoon salt
½ teaspoon pepper

This Arthur Family Winter Ritual recipe has been in my personal cookbook collection for over 30 years. Dean Campbell, a member of our church near Pittsburgh, brought us this delicious soup just before our daughter Amy was born in 1968. To this day, the title remains a mystery – president of what?

Cover dry limas with water and soak overnight. Next day, drain; remove skins and sprouts from beans; discard; set aside. Grate or shred vegetables; simmer in a small amount of water until just done; set aside. In separate pot, cover peeled limas with about 1 inch of water and simmer until just done. Combine vegetables with limas; add remaining ingredients. Simmer until well blended, usually about 30 minutes. Depending on the amount of liquid used, this recipe makes about one-half gallon of soup. Serve with corn bread and applesauce. Keeps well in freezer for a quick homemade soup "hankering." Popping the bean skins is time-consuming, but the result is worth the time. Serves 10.

She-Crab or Sook Soup

One to two 8-ounce cans crabmeat
One 10¾-ounce can cream of chicken soup
One 10½-ounce can She-Crab soup
Dash of sherry

Pour crabmeat into bowl and with fingers, check for pieces of shell and cartilage. The quantity of crabmeat is a personal preference, but do not use the imitation crab. Mix all ingredients together in covered saucepan, and heat thoroughly over low heat. If desired, add more sherry but there should be just a "hint" of it. Serves 4.

Yes, there is a "he" crab and a "she" crab. Abdomen markings and claw colors distinguish the two crabs. The male crab or "Jimmy" has a Washington Monument shaped marking on the abdomen, and his claws are blue. The mature female crab or "Sook" has a U.S. Capitol shaped marking on her apron or abdomen, and her bright red claw tips look like she paints her fingernails.

In having moved to 6 states, we've not only experienced different climates, scenery and lifestyles, but different cuisines — and — different seafood! This She-Crab Soup recipe was shared with me by a member of Shandon Presbyterian Church in Columbia, Rubye Philson, who with her husband P.J. or "Doc" adopted us as family and included us on many social events. Rubye as a "Pearl Mesta" extraordinaire, taught me how to plan, coordinate, execute and, above all, enjoy giving dinner parties, receptions, and special-event parties. She especially delighted in spontaneous "do's." What a pair those two were!

Soup a L'oignon
(French Onion Soup)

8 small onions, peeled and thinly sliced in rings
3 tablespoons butter
2 heaping tablespoons all-purpose flour
7 cups (six 10½-ounce cans) beef consommé
Salt and pepper
Eight 1" to 1½" slices of French baguette
Parmesan cheese
8 Swiss cheese slices

In large saucepan sauté onions in butter 'till soft and golden. Sprinkle with flour; stir and cook 1 to 2 minutes. Slowly stir in consommé; salt and pepper to taste. Note: Soup has sodium/salt in it, so adjust in increments. Simmer 15 minutes. Place one slice of bread in each ovenproof bowl. Next, ladle soup to almost top of bowl. Sprinkle generously with Parmesan cheese. Top with slice of Swiss cheese and broil until cheese is melted and top is browned. Serves 8.

E-Z Grapefruit Salad

I requested this recipe after eating it at a dinner of one of our "Most Unforgettable Characters" in Harrisburg, Arlene Hershey. The daughter of Eli N. Hershey, a pioneer of the ice cream industry and founder of the Hershey Ice Cream Company around 1910, she was filled with stories of her days of professional singing in synagogues and Riverside Church in New York City, of working in the Special Services of the USO in the Philippines in 1947 writing and performing dramatic and musical productions for the troops. She returned to Harrisburg and sat on the Board of Directors of WMSP, a non-profit radio station owned by her church, Market Square Presbyterian, and became very active and supportive of local cultural events. Her quick wit and eagerness to enjoy every day of life were contagious.

Iceberg and Romaine lettuces, torn into bite-size pieces
Prepared red grapefruit sections in glass jar or cans
Avocados, optional
Sweet onion, thinly sliced and separated into rings
Roquefort cheese

Dressing:

⅔ part vegetable oil
⅓ part red wine vinegar
Sugar to taste
Garlic powder to taste

On salad plates, arrange lettuce pieces. Top with drained grapefruit sections and avocado slices. Add a few separated rings of onion and desired amount of crumbled Roquefort cheese. Drizzle dressing over salad and serve. Serves 6.

With the already-prepared grapefruit sections, this salad can be fixed in a "snap."

Caesar East Salad

4 slices Rye bread
Butter, softened
Garlic powder
1 large bunch Romaine lettuce
1 head Escarole lettuce
1 block Muenster cheese
1 red onion

Dressing:

⅔ cup oil
⅓ cup red wine vinegar
Grated Romano cheese
2 teaspoons regular mustard
Salt and freshly ground black pepper

To make croutons: Spread each piece of Rye bread with butter and sprinkle with garlic powder. Toast on one side. Remove from oven and prepare other side of bread; return to oven and toast that side. When cooled, cut into cubes; set aside.   In pint jar, combine dressing ingredients; shake well and set aside. Wash and dry torn pieces of lettuces and place in salad bowl. Add cubes of Muenster cheese and thin slices of red onion. At serving time toss with enough dressing to coat lettuce; add croutons. Any leftover dressing keeps well in refrigerator. Serves 4 to 6.

Honey of a Spinach Salad

⅓ cup vegetable oil
2½ tablespoons Dijon mustard
2½ tablespoons red wine vinegar
2½ tablespoons water
½ cup honey
⅓ cup walnuts, toasted and broken into pieces
3 slices bacon
One 10-ounce bag fresh spinach
½ head radicchio
1 bunch watercress

Combine oil and mustard with a wire whisk; stir in vinegar and water. Add honey, whisking until ingredients are well blended. Stir in walnuts. Cover and chill. Fry or microwave bacon, drain and crumble; set aside. Wash spinach, radicchio and watercress; dry with paper towels or in salad spinner. Combine all ingredients just before serving. Serves 6 to 8.

Cold Chinese Noodle Salad

One whole boneless chicken breast, cooked
5 ounces boiled or baked ham or 1 pound medium
shrimp, cooked and shelled
1 bunch green onions, cut in 2-inch lengths
1 pound Chinese rice stick noodles, vermicelli or
angel hair pasta
½ cup walnuts, coarsely chopped by hand
1½ cups vegetable oil
2½ tablespoons oriental sesame oil
2 tablespoons sesame seeds
3 tablespoons ground coriander
¾ cup soy sauce
Scant teaspoon chili oil

We gals always joked that our Book Club was just a reason to get together, visit and eat. Lots of great recipes were shared within that group, one of which was Nancy Spieser's noodle salad. The Chinese rice stick noodles, oriental sesame oil and chili oil may be found in specialty stores or oriental sections of most large grocery chains.

Cut chicken breast, ham and onions in julienne strips. In pot of boiling water, cook Chinese rice stick or pasta until done; drain. Combine in large bowl with chicken, ham or shrimp, green onions and walnuts. In medium skillet combine vegetable, sesame oil and sesame seeds, heating until seeds are lightly brown. Remove from heat, and cautiously stir in ground coriander and soy sauce. Add chili oil. Pour over salad and toss 'till thoroughly coated. Refrigerate at least 3 hours. If not using shrimp, it's even better a few days later.

Oriental Broccoli Slaw

Mary Barry is a retired professor of Fashion Merchandising at Auburn University and is always sharing fascinating stories of her worldwide adventures with her students and of her encounters with famous designers. In February 1995, for my one-week visit to Harrisburg before moving in May, Mary felt my short wool coat inadequate, so she freely loaned me her full-length mink coat with Armani shoulder pads. I spent most of my visit explaining why a minister's wife was wearing a mink coat! What an experience — what generosity!

1 cup slivered almonds, toasted
1 cup salted sunflower kernels
Two 3-ounce packages Oriental flavor Ramen noodles
16 ounces broccoli slaw
1 cup sliced green onion

Dressing:

¾ cup oil
¼ cup white vinegar
⅓ cup sugar
2 packets Ramen noodle seasoning

Ahead of time: Toast the almonds and combine with the sunflower nuts and crushed, uncooked noodles; set aside. Combine all dressing ingredients in a jar and shake well. Set aside. Combine the broccoli slaw and onions. Refrigerate. An hour before serving, add dressing to the slaw mixture and stir well. Just before serving, add the almonds, nuts, noodle mixture. Serves 6 to 8.

Salt Shakers Salad

Field greens or any combination salad greens
Mandarin oranges, drained
Golden raisins
Raisins
Dried cranberries
Oriental Orange Citrus Splash salad dressing
Walnut pieces, slightly toasted
Pecan pieces, toasted
Sliced or slivered almonds, toasted

Kay Bennett, a member at Eastminster Presbyterian Church in Stone Mountain, served this salad at one of our Salt Shakers dinners. Salt Shakers is one method this church uses to break a large congregation into smaller groups for fellowship by sharing a monthly meal and some chitchat. This recipe was a winner!! It's a great salad for Thanksgiving Day as a switch from the traditional congealed cranberry salad.

Wash greens and towel or spin dry. Place on individual salad plates. Arrange mandarin orange slices around greens. Sprinkle raisins and cranberries over salad. Drizzle with salad dressing. Sprinkle with walnuts, pecans and almonds. Servings and quantities depend on amount desired.

Oriental Chicken Salad

½ pound fresh spinach, washed and dried
6 chicken breasts, cooked and cut into chunks
One 8-ounce package fresh mushroom slices,
washed
3 green onions, sliced thinly
One 11-ounce can Mandarin orange sections,
drained
½ cup slivered almonds, toasted
2 tablespoons sesame seeds, toasted
One 3-ounce can chow mein noodles

Dressing:

¼ cup tarragon vinegar
¼ cup vegetable oil
2 tablespoons sugar
2 teaspoons salt

Tear spinach into bite-size pieces and toss together with next 6 ingredients. Refrigerate. Combine dressing ingredients in a jar, shaking to mix thoroughly. At serving time, add dressing to spinach mixture. Sprinkle with chow mein noodles.

Artichoke and Rice Salad

One 8-ounce package chicken Rice-A-Roni
One 6-ounce jar marinated artichokes
4 green onions, thinly sliced
½ green pepper, chopped
12 stuffed green olives, sliced
1 cup or more diced cooked shrimp or
grilled chicken
½ cup mayonnaise
¾ teaspoon curry powder

For those of us where curry was not our native cooking spice, it's an acquired taste. Be adventurous — try it more than once and you'll be "hooked." There's never a morsel left of this salad, Jackie Lunsford tells me.

Cook Rice-A-Roni according to directions, omitting butter; cool. Drain artichokes, reserving marinade. Cut artichokes in half and add to rice, together with onions, green pepper and olives. Add diced cooked shrimp or grilled chicken. In separate bowl, combine mayonnaise, curry powder and reserved artichoke marinade. Toss with rice mixture and chill. Serves 6.

Walnut & Watercress Salad

1 cup walnut halves
1 bunch watercress, washed and dried,
tough stems removed
1 apple, peeled, cored and diced
¼ cup (2 ounces) diced Gruyère cheese
2 teaspoons chopped Spanish onion
8 ripe olives
3 eggs, hard-boiled and halved

Walnut Oil Vinaigrette:

½ cup walnut oil
1 tablespoon red wine vinegar
½ teaspoon Dijon mustard
Kosher salt and fresh ground pepper

In salad bowl combine all salad ingredients. Toss gently. Make vinaigrette dressing and pour on salad. Toss thoroughly and serve. Serves 4.

Corned Beef Salad or Sandwich Filling

One 12-ounce can corned beef
Two hard-boiled eggs, chopped
½ cup chopped green olives
¼ cup finely chopped onion
1 cup grated sharp Cheddar cheese
1½ tablespoon Worcestershire sauce
2 tablespoons horseradish
Salt and pepper to taste
½ to ¾ cup catsup or mayonnaise or a combination

In large bowl break corned beef apart with fork; add remaining ingredients, mix well. Serve on lettuce leaf as a luncheon salad or place in hamburger bun. For a hot sandwich, wrap filled bun in foil and heat in 375° oven for 10 to 15 minutes. I have even used this recipe for a party as a spread for plain crackers.

In the mid-1960's, Bill's first staff pastorate was in Clarksburg. Two or three active church families took this bachelor under their wings. One family was Paul and Lil Gordon who, almost 40 years later, have never stopped caring and supporting us. Lil is a marvelous cook both at home and for church groups and is a genuine caregiver. Lil's recipe for this salad has been altered with my own addition of hard-boiled eggs.

Fried Green Tomatoes Sandwich

Two slices fried green tomatoes per sandwich
Buttermilk
Egg
Corn meal
Peanut oil
Challah or French bread
2 slices bacon, fried crisp
Mozzarella cheese
Lettuce
1000 Island Dressing

Another version is to place thoroughly cooked hamburger patty on bun; top with fried green tomato slices; then goat cheese. Place in broiler until cheese melts; remove and top with red pepper sauce and top of bun. Note: Fried Green Tomatoes are best known as a side item but make a delicious and change-of-pace sandwich.

Choose green tomatoes that are turning slightly red but are still very firm. Slice in ½-inch slices and soak in buttermilk for several hours. Make egg wash with beaten egg and small amount of buttermilk. Dip in egg wash, then into deep amount of cornmeal. Fry immediately in 1-inch of hot peanut oil. Flip only once to fry second side. Transfer to paper toweling. On thick slice of bread, place tomato, bacon and cheese; broil 'till cheese is melted; remove and top with lettuce and a dollop of 1000 Island Dressing. Tabasco may be added to dressing for "extra kick." Eat open faced or with top bread slice.

Seaburgers

Two 7-ounce cans tuna, drained
½ cup chopped celery
¼ cup dry bread crumbs
⅔ cup Marzetti's cole slaw dressing, no substitute
2 tablespoons chopped parsley
2 tablespoons instant minced onions
Dash of salt and pepper
½ to ¾ stick margarine
8 hamburger buns, toasted

This recipe is from my pre-teen collection era — so it's an "antique recipe" now.

Combine first 8 ingredients. Shape into 8 patties; lightly coat with additional dry bread crumbs. If time permits, refrigerate to solidify and make them hold together better. Melt margarine in skillet over medium heat; sauté patty until heated through and browned on both sides. Place hot patty on bottom of toasted bun. Top with processed cheese slice and top of bun and broil until cheese melts.

Shrimp or Chicken Poo-Pah's

While visiting New Orleans in 1987 with our friends, the Freundts from Jackson, Mississippi, we ordered Shrimp Poo Pah's at the Acme Oyster Bar. What a new find! The next year while visiting our Latvian friend, Via Wilson, in Tennessee, Bill mentioned this sandwich. Her recipe for New Orleans Barbecued Shrimp was IT! Our son David often substitutes chicken for the shrimp.

Small French bread loaves, usually 6 to a package
3 to 4 pounds raw shrimp, in shells or
2 pounds bite-size chicken chunks
½ teaspoon ground black pepper
½ teaspoon cayenne pepper
½ teaspoon celery salt
1 teaspoon salt
½ cup Worcestershire sauce
3 tablespoons olive oil
1 tablespoon thyme
1 tablespoon garlic powder
1 tablespoon parsley flakes
1 stick real butter
1 teaspoon rosemary, crushed

Divide each small loaf in half, hollow out soft bread of loaf, leaving about ½ inch of bread inside crust to absorb sauce. Heat at 350° about 5 minutes until crusty. Set aside. Shell shrimp; refrigerate. In saucepan combine the remaining ingredients and bring to boil. Add shrimp and cook 3 minutes. If using chicken, cook until done. Note: Cooking time cannot be accurately provided since it depends on size of chunks. Spoon into bread shells. Serve with cole slaw and extra napkins! Serves 6 to 12.

Strombolli

1 loaf frozen bread dough
8-ounce package boiled ham
8-ounce Genoa salami
8-ounce package Mozzarella slices
8-ounce package Swiss cheese
2 tablespoons all-purpose flour
Cooking oil spray
Solid butter for crust after baking
Spaghetti or pizza sauce

Cousin-in-law from McClellandtown, Pennsylvania, Lois Vaccaro, demonstrated this loaf one year while visiting us. It's always well received — and — devoured!

Thaw bread and set aside. Cut meats and cheeses in 1½-inch strips. Flour breadboard or counter and roll out bread to a 12 x10 inch rectangle. Lengthwise, leaving a ½-inch border at both ends, place ham strips down the center; top with Mozzarella cheese strips; then with salami strips; last, layer with Swiss cheese strips. Bring long sides of bread dough together and seal by pressing securely. Spray cookie sheet and place loaf, sealed side down on sheet. Bake at 375° for 30 minutes. Remove from oven and with stick of solid butter, rub the top of the crust. Slice into 2-inch slices and spoon sauce over the slice. This baked loaf freezes well; just thaw on cookie sheet, cover loosely with tin foil and reheat at 350° for 10 minutes. Serve with tossed salad. Serves 3 to 4.

Indoor Grill Veggie Wrap

Paige Parsons has other indoor grill recipes in the Breakfast & Brunch and Entrées sections of this cookbook.

One 28-ounce bag frozen stir-fry vegetable mix
2 to 3 Portabello mushrooms
1 medium zucchini
½ medium eggplant
¼ cup Balsamic vinegar
6 large flour tortillas

Preheat indoor grill 5 minutes. In bowl toss frozen vegetable mix and other vegetables with Balsamic vinegar. Place vegetables on grill and grill 5 minutes. Note: Your favorite vegetables may be substituted for those listed. To make more pliable, warm tortillas in microwave a few seconds and fill with vegetable mix. It's a wrap!

Side Items

Peach

Amy's Favorite Orange Baked Beans

This is one of those favorite childhood recipes our daughter Amy has taken from our home to her home. Now as a busy stay-at-home mom with two little girls, she enjoys whipping out mom's easy recipes. Switching from career woman as an industrial engineer manager to full-time mom was quite a transition. Amy continually uses her musical talents but has discovered so many creative talents she never realized she possessed. It's so heartwarming and rewarding when parents see what great parents their children become for their grandchildren.

One 1-pound 15-ounce can baked beans
½ cup brown sugar
¼ cup catsup
3 tablespoons frozen orange juice concentrate, thawed
1 tablespoon dehydrated minced onion
½ teaspoon Worcestershire sauce

Stir all ingredients together. Bring to boiling point, reduce heat and simmer uncovered for 10 minutes. Serves 4 to 6. It's always a winner at a picnic!

Garlic Grits Casserole

1 cup regular grits
4 cups water
1 teaspoon salt
One 6-ounce roll Kraft garlic cheese
One-half 6-ounce roll Kraft garlic cheese
2 ounces sharp Cheddar cheese
1 stick margarine
½ cup milk
1 cup sour cream
3 eggs, well beaten
1 cup crushed corn flake crumbs
One-half 6-ounce roll Kraft garlic cheese

For some 30 years Mary Daniels was an institution at the First United Presbyterian Church in my hometown. As its secretary and administrator, she provided lots of formality and order to the congregation and guided one fresh-from-seminary pastor, my Bill. As a very special friend, we were her extended family. Whenever she knew our son David was coming for dinner, she'd feature his favorite — Garlic Grits Casserole.

Cook grits, water and salt according to directions for 35 minutes. Mixture will be thick. Stir in 1½ rolls garlic cheese, sharp Cheddar cheese and margarine; cool this mixture then add milk and sour cream; add eggs. Pour into buttered, flat 3-quart glass casserole. Top with 1 cup crumbs and dot with butter and thin slices of last half of second roll of garlic cheese. This dish can be refrigerated at this point, brought to room temperature and baked. Bake at 350° for 45 minutes.

Baked Fresh Asparagus

2 pounds fresh asparagus
3 tablespoons minced fresh parsley
2 tablespoons olive oil
2 tablespoons melted butter
Salt and pepper to taste

Wash, drain and break off tough white ends of asparagus spears. Arrange in one layer, if possible, in flat glass casserole. Sprinkle with parsley. Combine the oil and melted butter and drizzle over the asparagus, then add salt and pepper. Cover baking dish with aluminum foil and bake at 400° for 15 minutes. If you must arrange asparagus in two layers, increase time to 25 minutes. Serves 6.

Caramelized Carrots

Two 16-ounce bags frozen crinkle carrots,
cooked and drained
6 slices bacon, fried and crumbled, reserving grease
1 medium onion, chopped and sautéed
in bacon grease
2 cups brown sugar

Butter 2-quart casserole. Keep layering carrots, then brown sugar; then bacon, until all ingredients are used. Bake in 350° oven for 1 hour, stirring every 15 minutes to caramelize.

Tailgating Marinated Broccoli

1 bunch broccoli

⅓ cup cider vinegar

½ cup vegetable oil

1 teaspoon dried dill weed

1 teaspoon sugar

1 teaspoon Accent (MSG)

¼ slightly heaping teaspoon salt

¼ slightly heaping teaspoon garlic salt

¼ slightly heaping teaspoon freshly ground pepper

As a young bride and pastor's wife, Dora Faye Smith was quite a role model for me. She is my longest - not my oldest! - cooking buddy. We shared many happy times in the Springtime of our marriage with her, her husband Paul who was a Methodist pastor, and their two children.

Cut broccoli into flowerettes and cut the stalks into strips. Wash and drain. In large jar or bowl mix the remaining ingredients. Close container and shake 'till marinade is well blended. Add broccoli pieces to marinade, shake to coat, and place in refrigerator. Marinate for 12 to 24 hours, shaking container two or three times.

Note: This is a marvelous addition to a vegetable tray or wonderful for tailgating, picnics or "finger food" occasions. Use a half-gallon upright jar for easy storage and shaking. Upright containers take less shelf space in the refrigerator that always seems to be bulging.

Elegant Rice Casserole

A missionary after serving 40 years in China was asked where he intended to spend retirement. When he answered, "… in South Carolina," he was asked, "Why there?" He replied, "It's about as close to China as I could get in that they eat a lot of rice and they worship their ancestors!"

1 cup regular rice

2½ cups water

3 chicken bouillon cubes

One 2.25-ounce package slivered almonds, toasted

One 10-ounce package frozen tiny peas, partially cooked

¼ cup chopped onion

½ teaspoon curry powder

½ teaspoon white pepper

3 tablespoons liquid Italian dressing

1 cup chopped celery

½ cup mayonnaise

½ cup Italian dressing

Cook rice in water with bouillon cubes until tender. Mix all ingredients together and place in 9 x 13-inch long, flat casserole. Bake at 300° for 30 minutes or if refrigerated, for 40 minutes. Delicious served hot or at room temperature. Serves 8 to 10.

Note: At Christmas time I use one 2-ounce jar of pimientos, drained.

Fresh Tomato Pie

One 9-inch pie crust
5 to 6 fresh, ripe tomatoes or 8 to 10 Roma's,
thickly sliced
One ½-ounce plastic package of fresh basil,
cut with scissors
4 to 5 tablespoons chopped fresh chives
¾ cup mayonnaise
1 ½ cups shredded Cheddar cheese

My friend, Jackie Lunsford, "snazzes up" a serving plate with a wedge of this tomato pie. Its visual shape, bright colors and "fresh-from-the-garden" aroma can't be surpassed.

Using deep-dish glass pie plate, form pie crust and partially bake, according to directions. Visually divide tomato slices, basil and chives and layer each item until crust is filled. In bowl mix mayonnaise and Cheddar cheese. Spread on last layer. Sprinkle with additional Cheddar cheese. Bake in 400° oven for 35 minutes. Serves 6 to 8.

Grandma VanHorn's E-Z Old-Fashioned Succotash

Grandma VanHorn loved to cook and took great pride in her garden produce and picture-perfect pantry filled with canned vegetables, fruits and stew meat. To prepare for Sunday's dinner, she would ring the necks of 2 or 3 chickens on Saturday, pluck the feathers after dipping them in boiling water, then singe any remaining down, cut up the chickens and begin frying. The more folks around her table, the merrier. My family tells me I inherited her joy of cooking and entertaining... plus some characteristics that become more evident with age!

2 cups chopped celery
1 cup chopped onion
6 to 8 tablespoons melted butter, divided
One 17-ounce can lima beans, drained
One 12-ounce can corn, drained
Salt and pepper

In large skillet, sauté celery and onion in 3 tablespoons butter until tender. Add beans and corn. Add remaining butter and season to taste with salt and pepper; heat thoroughly. Serves 4 to 6.

Grandma Mary's Scalloped or Au Gratin Potatoes

Bill's mother Mary's Scalloped Potatoes has become a trademark dish for our family. It is relatively inexpensive, easy and complements so many entrées. It is difficult for the younger generation to realize that in pre-frozen, pre-boxed, pre-fast-food, yea pre-historic, days, most all food was prepared from "scratch" until the mid-1900's.

For scalloped potatoes:

One 10¾-ounce can cream of mushroom soup
¼ cup milk
6 to 8 regular potatoes, peeled and thinly sliced
1 to 2 onions, thinly sliced
All-purpose flour
Butter
Salt and pepper
One 2.5-ounce or larger jar of mushrooms, drained
Milk

For au gratin potatoes:

Omit mushrooms, mushroom soup and milk;
substitute 1½ to 2 cups shredded Cheddar cheese

Generously butter 2-quart glass baking dish. In small bowl combine mushroom soup and ¼ cup milk. Set aside. In casserole place a single layer of potatoes, add a single layer of onions, sprinkle sparingly with flour — this helps to thicken sauce — dot with butter, salt and pepper. Pour on a portion of soup mixture; sprinkle with mushrooms. Repeat layers, ending with soup mixture. Fill casserole with milk just slightly over last layer. Bake at 350° until fork inserts easily through potatoes. The baking time will depend upon casserole size and thickness of slices.

Quantity of potatoes and onions may have to be adjusted, depending on size.

Orange Beets

2 tablespoons cornstarch
1¼ cups light brown sugar
One 6-ounce can frozen orange juice concentrate
6 ounces reserved beet liquid
¾ cup cider vinegar
1 tablespoon butter
Three 15-ounce cans small whole beets, drained,
reserving liquid

Combine thoroughly cornstarch and sugar in saucepan. Blend in orange juice concentrate, then beet liquid and vinegar. Cook over medium heat, stirring constantly, until mixture is thick and clear. Add butter and beets, reheat and serve or place in double boiler over simmering water to keep hot 'till serving time. This dish may be prepared the day before. Reheat slowly over hot water or on medium microwave power. Serves 12 but recipe may be halved.

Note: Press the combined cornstarch and sugar through a sieve with spoon or spurtle (a Scottish kitchen utensil which resembles a wooden spoon handle used for stirring porridge).

Quick Butternut Squash

1 butternut squash
Honey

Peel and cut in chunks one butternut squash and place in saucepan with about ½ inch of water. Slowly simmer until the squash is fork tender. Spear one piece of squash at a time and transfer to serving dish, then mash. When all pieces are mashed, stir in desired amount of honey, tasting as you add. This is such a good source of beta-carotene and adds a bright spot on a serving plate.

When our friend John Sasek comes to visit, he loves preparing our meals … and so do we! He is a rare breed in that he concocts his own original recipes that are always fantastic! "Come more often, John" are always our parting words.

Corn Pudding

Margaret Wiltshire is among our "Unforgettable Characters" from Richmond days. Visiting her home filled with her own handmade furniture where she had lived for over half a century was such fun for our family. She delighted in showing our children how to bake biscuits on her wood-burning stove while always having something like this Corn Pudding baking in her "modern oven." The visit's highlight was being swept up in her marvelous stories from days of "yore" and recent travels. From comforting little David in his fear of the dark to checking herself from a nursing facility to fly with a caretaker to Columbia for Amy's wedding, Margaret was a family treasure.

2 heaping tablespoons all-purpose flour
¼ cup sugar
1 teaspoon salt
½ teaspoon pepper
4 eggs, beaten
Two 15-ounce cans cream-style corn
One 11-ounce whole corn, drained
1¼ cups milk
¼ cup butter, softened
2 tablespoons butter

Mix together the dry ingredients. In separate bowl beat eggs and add corn, milk and softened butter; stir in dry ingredients. Transfer to a buttered 2-quart casserole dish. Dot with chunks of butter. Set casserole in pan to which has been added water to 1-inch depth. The presence of water acts like a double boiler and will prevent sticking and provide moisture. It's recommended that the last 10 or 15 minutes of baking, remove pan of water and return casserole to finish baking. Bake in 350° oven until set; usually 1 to 1¼ hours. Serves 8.

Autumn Scottish Turnips & Apples

2 large turnips, peeled and sliced
2 tablespoons butter
2 cups peeled Granny Smith apple slices
½ teaspoon ground cinnamon

Crumb topping:

⅓ cup all-purpose flour
⅓ cup light brown sugar, packed
2 tablespoons butter, firm enough to cut in

While serving Tuckahoe Presbyterian Church in Richmond, a lovely Scottish "lass," Norma McClintic, introduced us to quite a few Scottish dishes — 25 years later, the Turnips and Apples dish remains one of our favorites. In Scotland, turnips are a food staple like potatoes or rice in the U.S. Their unique taste often receives "bad press" but this recipe will change that label, I promise.

Place turnips in saucepan with water and cook 'till tender. Drain and mash with fork or mixer and add butter. Butter one 9-inch square glass pan. Layer turnips and apples, ending with apples. Sprinkle with cinnamon. Make crumb topping by mixing flour and brown sugar; cut in the butter with a fork or pastry blender until mixture is crumbly. Scatter on top of turnip and apple layers. Bake at 350° for 1 hour. Serves 4 to 6.

Amaretto Hot Fruit Compote

Louisiana born and bred George Wilkes, a retired landscape architect now living in Atlanta, is a creative and avid cook. He and Royetta always served this compote at their bountiful Cajun New Year's Eve celebration. Our long-time friendship with George's son has blessed us with this extension of our circle of friends.

One 16-ounce can peach halves
One 16-ounce can pear halves
One 15¼-ounce can pineapple chunks
One 17-ounce can apricot halves
One 16½-ounce can pitted dark sweet cherries
2 bananas, sliced
1 teaspoon lemon juice
12 soft coconut macaroons, crumbled
One 2.25-ounce package sliced almonds,
toasted and divided
4 tablespoons butter
⅓ cup amaretto or almond flavored liqueur or
1 to 2 teaspoons almond extract

Drain and gently mix first 5 ingredients. In small bowl gently mix banana slices with lemon juice. Fold into fruit mixture. In long 2½ to 3-quart casserole layer one half of combined fruits and one half of macaroon crumbs. Sprinkle with 3 tablespoons sliced toasted almonds and dot with 2 tablespoons butter. Repeat using last half of fruit and macaroons and butter. Pour amaretto over mixture. Bake uncovered at 350° for 30 minutes. Sprinkle with remaining almonds. Gently stir mixture before serving. Serves 10 to 12 but recipe can be easily halved.

Note: This compote is delicious for a brunch or with pork, chicken or ham entrées.

Showy Broccoli Sunburst

Two 10-ounce boxes frozen broccoli spears,
partially cooked
2 tablespoons butter, melted
1 tablespoon lemon juice
2 egg whites, room temperature
Pinch of cream of tartar
⅓ cup mayonnaise
2 tablespoons or more grated sharp Cheddar cheese
Paprika for garnish

While broccoli is cooking, combine butter and lemon juice. Preheat broiler 10 minutes. Place rack on lowest shelf. With mixer, beat egg whites and add cream of tartar; beat on high until stiff peaks form. Fold in mayonnaise. Set aside. Drain broccoli. In a 10-inch glass pie pan, place broccoli stem ends towards middle with flower ends at edge of pie pan. Pour lemon butter over flower ends. Heap mound of egg white mixture in center over stems. Sprinkle with cheese and paprika. Broil 2 to 3 minutes or until egg whites are set. Voila — a golden sunburst!

Suth'rn Per'low
(Southern Pilaf)

A bit of etymology:
Pilau, pilaw, pilaff appears in
English in many terms
according to the language or
locality of the writer or cook.
In the South, many adopted
the pronunciation per'low.
The earlier examples from
17th century Turkish are
identical to the Persian one of
pilaw mentioned in a 1426
writing. In the *Oxford* dic-
tionary it is defined as "an
Oriental dish consisting of
rice boiled with fowl or fish
and spices, raisins, etc."

One 4-pound whole chicken, washed thoroughly
Celery leaves
Bay leaf
Salt and pepper
½ pound hot sausage
½ pound mild sausage
2 cups regular rice
1 cup chicken broth
Black pepper

Place chicken in large pot and cover with water; add seasonings. Bring liquid to a boil, reduce heat and simmer 1 hour or
until chicken is done. Remove bay leaf and chicken and let
cool; debone chicken. Strain and reserve broth. Set aside. In
skillet completely cook both sausages over medium low heat.
Drain and set aside. About 30 minutes before serving, cook
rice according to package directions. Combine all ingredients
and sprinkle liberally with ground black pepper. Serves 6 to
8. A great accompaniment for all varieties of barbecue.

Sweet Potato Fries

2 large sweet potatoes
Peanut oil
Salt and pepper

Peel sweet potatoes and cut into strips the size of favorite French fries. Heat peanut oil until hot enough to make a "test" sweet potato strip fry quickly or at recommended temperature on French fryer. When fries are finished, remove and drain on paper towel. Sprinkle with salt and pepper. These reheat in a 350° oven for 3 to 5 minutes. Serves 2 to 3.

Sweet potatoes are a great source of beta carotene, a necessary body nutrient … and a switch from white potatoes!

Variation: If you can slice the sweet potatoes thinly, follow the same procedure and make sweet potato chips!

Caramelized Vidalia Onions

Georgia is the land of Vidalia onions. Next to peaches, there's hardly anything more Georgian. Our friend, Bernard Blackwell, from Eastminster Presbyterian Church in Stone Mountain, has come near to perfecting the use of Vidalia onions in this delightful recipe he shared with us. There are never any leftovers!

4 Vidalia onions or any sweet onions
4 teaspoons solid butter
4 beef bouillon cubes
4 tablespoons brown sugar
Cinnamon
Honey

Peel onions and core not quite all the way through, making a well in the center. Slightly cut some gashes in top of onion to absorb seasonings. Put 1 teaspoon solid butter in each onion; add 1 beef bouillon cube in the center. Pack 1 tablespoon brown sugar on top of each onion and sprinkle with 3 shakes of ground cinnamon; then drizzle with honey. Cover with aluminum foil and bake at 350° for 30 minutes or longer. When long-tined fork inserts easily, the onions are cooked. Serves 4.

Vidalias with a Kick

4 Vidalia onions or any sweet onions
4 teaspoons solid butter
Worcestershire sauce to taste

This is a wonderful accompaniment to steak or hamburgers and is so very easy!

Peel onions and core, making a well in the center. Slightly cut some gashes in top of onion to absorb butter and Worcestershire sauce. Put 1 teaspoon solid butter in each onion and pour Worcestershire sauce over each onion. Cover with aluminum foil and bake at 350° for 30 minutes or longer. When long-tined fork inserts easily, the onions are cooked. Serves 4.

Cabbage with Glazed Onions

1 head cabbage
Salt and pepper
4 thick slices bacon
1 jar pearl onions

Another Tom Summers' recipe via e-mail — we could almost smell it on the monitor! Cabbage is one of our family's main vegetables so a new "twist" is always welcomed.

Cut cabbage in bite-size pieces and place in kettle with water. Season with salt and pepper. Boil for 15 minutes over medium-high heat until cabbage is translucent but not completely cooked. It should be crunchy when pierced with a fork. While cabbage is cooking, fry bacon in skillet, reserving about ¼ cup grease; drain bacon on paper towels. Drain jar of onions and glaze in bacon grease. Drain cabbage and add to skillet. Quickly toss and sauté for a few minutes. Serves about 5 or 6.

Redskin Mashed Potatoes

Frequently while we're on-line, an e-mail from Tom Summers will flash on our screen. Tom, a native of Clarksburg, now lives in Washington, DC, but we've known him for over 35 years. He enjoys eating and likes to cook and share his "finds" with us like these potatoes we prepared and now serve often.

10 to 12 uniform-size red potatoes
2 to 3 garlic cloves, thinly sliced
Salt and pepper
½ to ¾ stick real butter
½ to ¾ cup sour cream

Add water to saucepan or pot. Scrub, but do not peel, potatoes; remove any blemishes. Boil whole potatoes and garlic until thoroughly cooked. Drain water off potatoes. Do not completely mash potatoes and garlic, seasoning with salt and pepper and butter. Lumpy potatoes are "in," especially in the larger cities.

Variation: Peel and cut up one small rutabaga; cook with the potatoes and mash together. This is a variegated side item and quite eye-catching.

Green Beans a là Dijon

4 large handfuls of fresh green beans
1 to 2 tablespoons Dijon mustard, in increments
Vermouth, optional

Wash and snap off stem end of green beans. Leave beans whole. Arrange beans in steamer over water to which 2 tablespoons of inexpensive Vermouth has been added and steam until the beans are crisp-tender; drain well. Fold in Dijon mustard, coating the beans. Note: Add mustard gradually since size of beans affect mustard needed. Vermouth in the steaming water keeps green beans, asparagus and broccoli a brighter green.

This recipe comes by way of a neighbor on West Club Lane in Richmond and a dear friend for almost 30 years, Mary Jane Wiecking. Our children were in each other's home many times each week. Mary Jane's "half-full glass" outlook on life was infectious, her spirit of community made these "new kids on the block" feel right at home, and her dependability was comforting.

Zucchini Fans

for Non-Fans of Zucchini

Want a vegetable that makes a statement? This is it!

⅓ cup butter, softened
2 tablespoons minced fresh parsley
½ teaspoon dried whole tarragon
⅛ teaspoon salt
⅛ teaspoon pepper
4 small zucchini, no larger than 2 inches in diameter
¼ cup water
2 tablespoons freshly grated Parmesan cheese
1 tablespoon soft breadcrumbs

Combine butter, parsley, tarragon, salt and pepper; set aside. Cut each zucchini into lengthwise slices, leaving slices attached on stem end. Fan out slices, spreading evening with butter mixture. Place in a 15 x 10 x 1" jellyroll pan; add water. Bake at 400° for 20 minutes or until crisp-tender. Combine Parmesan cheese and crumbs; sprinkle on zucchini; broil 4 inches from heat for 2 minutes or until cheese melts. Serves 4.

Entrées

Quince

Chicken Marsala with Mushrooms

My husband Bill ate Chicken Marsala in a Kentucky restaurant, dissecting each bite and re-creating it at home. Now he often prepares it for our dinner guests who always request the recipe. Except for cooking time, it's a 10-minute recipe.

Four 4-ounce boneless, skinless chicken breasts or cutlets
White wine for soaking chicken pieces
1 tablespoon vegetable oil
¼ cup flour, seasoned with salt and pepper
1 tablespoon vegetable oil
1 pound large white mushrooms
2 to 3 cloves garlic, crushed
½ cup dry Marsala wine
¾ cup chicken broth

Wash chicken pieces thoroughly, place in bowl or re-closeable plastic bag and cover with white wine. Refrigerate and let soak for at least 2 hours, then drain. Dredge drained chicken pieces in seasoned flour. In large nonstick skillet, heat 1 tablespoon oil; sauté chicken about 3 minutes per side or until cooked. Remove from skillet. Heat 1 tablespoon oil and sauté mushrooms and garlic until mushrooms brown, usually 6-8 minutes. Add Marsala and chicken broth and boil 2 minutes to thicken. Add chicken pieces; cover skillet and simmer 35-45 minutes. Serves 4.

A good menu with this entrée is tomato aspic, garlic mashed potatoes, and green beans.

E-Z Pot Poulet

One 10¾-ounce can cream of mushroom soup
One 6-ounce jar sliced mushrooms
1½ cups white wine
1 cup plus 2 tablespoons sour cream
4 halves skinless, boneless chicken breasts
Nutty-flavored rice, or white rice or noodles

In crockpot add soup, mushrooms, wine, sour cream and chicken breasts. Turn crockpot on high temperature for 30 minutes, then reduce heat to low and let cook for 8 hours. When ready to serve, prepare rice according to package directions. Top with mixture from crockpot. Serve with a fruit salad and poppy seed dressing or a garden salad with French or Catalina dressing. Vegetables could be peas and carrots mixed, green beans or asparagus. Serves 6 to 8.

After preparing numerous times, Caroline Alff contends that Taylor's Lake Country Wine is the "secret ingredient" for this recipe.

Caroline Alff and husband Karl entered our lives in 2001 as members of Eastminster Presbyterian Church in Stone Mountain. Whether it's surprising folks with something special, suggesting a good book or "nifty" places to eat, injecting chats with native South Carolina family expressions, Caroline provides lots of information, fun and laughter, and a good dose of reality. Loving to cook for her family and friends, she shares this easy dish that qualifies for gourmet classification.

Chicken & Cots

Thanks for this yummy, fruity chicken recipe goes to my spontaneous Harrisburg friend, Anna Johnston, who loves to entertain friends on the deck overlooking her spectacular flower garden she tends like a mother.

1 teaspoon seasoned salt
Pepper
¼ to ½ teaspoon paprika
½ cup all-purpose flour
4 chicken breasts halves, boned or
4 boneless chicken breasts
½ cup vegetable or canola oil
1 cup barbecue sauce

Mix together first 4 ingredients. Dust chicken with flour mixture and brown quickly in oil on both sides. Remove to baking pan and brush with barbecue sauce. Cover and bake in preheated 400° oven for 15 minutes. Remove cover and reduce oven to 350°.

While chicken is baking, prepare sauce:

1 stick butter
½ medium onion, chopped
¼ green pepper, chopped
2½ ounces crushed pineapple
8 ounces apricot jam or preserves
1 cup cooking sherry
Cooking juices from baked chicken breasts
16 dried apricot halves

In saucepan melt butter and add next 5 ingredients. Simmer for 20 minutes. Add the juices from the baked chicken and spoon sauce over chicken breasts. Arrange 3 or 4 apricot halves on each chicken breast.   Cover.   Return chicken to 350° and bake an additional 20 minutes. Serves 4.

Personal Preference: While boneless chicken breasts are quick to prepare, they are expensive and somehow don't have the same flavor. Learning how to cut up chicken will save you bucks. It just takes practice and a good, sharp boning knife.

Italian Chicken Breasts

4 deboned chicken breast halves, pounded
All-purpose flour
Salt and pepper
Olive oil
½ to ¾ cup white wine
2 tablespoons lemon juice
Fresh rosemary
2 to 3 cloves fresh garlic, minced
Capers, drained

In flat pan mix together flour, salt and pepper. Dredge chicken breasts in flour mixture and brown quickly in hot oil; remove from skillet and set aside. To skillet drippings add wine, lemon juice, desired amount of rosemary and garlic; add capers. Return browned chicken breasts to skillet; cover; reduce heat to simmer and cook until chicken is done, generally 35 to 45 minutes. This entrée is delicious served with sautéed vegetables mixed with cooked spaghetti. Serves 4.

Deviled Chicken

After cleaning the red carpet Jackie Lunsford always rolls out for her guests, she finds this easy entrée not only a timesaver but a gourmet's delight.

2 sticks margarine, melted
1 tablespoon dry mustard
1 tablespoon Worcestershire sauce
1 teaspoon Tabasco
1 tablespoon lemon juice
One 14-ounce package herbed dressing
8 chicken breasts, deboned

Combine first 5 ingredients in deep bowl. Roll herbed dressing to make finer crumbs and place in aluminum pie plate or flat dish. Dip chicken in butter mixture, then roll in crumbs. Place in long, flat casserole. Cover with foil and bake at 300° for 1½ hours. Broil if not brown enough. This dish is delicious served with Elegant Rice (see Side Items section). Serves 8.

King Midas Chicken

1 whole chicken, cut up or equivalent
1 teaspoon salt
One 8-ounce can crushed pineapple, undrained
¼ cup regular mustard
½ cup chutney
½ cup chopped walnuts or pecans

Wash chicken and pat dry. Sprinkle chicken with salt. Place chicken in shallow, long, flat casserole in single layer, skin side up. Mix together last 4 ingredients and spoon over chicken. Bake uncovered at 350° for 1 hour 25 minutes. Serves 4 to 6.

Chutney is a preserved, tangy fruit mixture usually found in the pickle section of a grocery store. It is used in many recipes in England and India and adds an extra special flavor to many dishes.

South-of-the-Border Chicken with Green Chilies

While living in Columbia, our friends, Randall and Susan Bridwell served us this tasty Tex-Mex grilled chicken. Although a law professor of Seamanship at the University of South Carolina, Randall hails from Texas and always enjoys preparing a dish from their unbeatable Tex-Mex recipe collection.

2 cloves garlic
Three 4.5-ounce cans chopped chilies
1 jalapeño pepper, seeds removed
2 teaspoons chopped fresh cilantro
3 tablespoons olive oil
3 tablespoons lemon juice
$\frac{1}{2}$ teaspoon ground cumin
$\frac{1}{2}$ teaspoon salt
$\frac{1}{4}$ teaspoon black pepper
4 chicken breasts, thighs or legs

Make marinade by puréeing all ingredients except chicken pieces. Pour into re-closeable plastic bag. Add washed chicken pieces to marinade and refrigerate all day or overnight. Bring chicken and marinade to room temperature. Prepare charcoal grill. Remove chicken from marinade and microwave on high for 10 minutes, turning several times. Transfer chicken to grill and baste with marinade often. Boil marinade for 10 minutes and pour over grilled chicken. Serves 4. Round out the menu with black beans and rice, fried plantains, and tossed salad with lemon and oil vinaigrette dressing.

Leftover Turkey Casserole

One or two 10-ounce boxes frozen broccoli spears,
partially cooked
Cooked turkey cut into large pieces
Shredded sharp Cheddar cheese
One 5-ounce can evaporated milk
One 10¾-ounce can cream of mushroom soup
Onion rings, frozen

Members of Eastminster Presbyterian Church in Marietta, Chuck and Rita Frew opened their doors and hearts to us when Bill was chosen as the interim pastor. Traveling extensively as owners of Frew Travel, quick meals, especially after holiday preparation, are essential to their lifestyle. Try this one with leftover Thanksgiving turkey.

For bottom layer, lay broccoli in casserole. Next, put layer of turkey. Cover generously with cheese. In small bowl mix together evaporated milk and soup. Pour over cheese layer. Bake in preheated 350° oven for 25 minutes. Remove and top with frozen onion rings. Return to oven for additional 5 minutes or until onion rings are browned. Serves 6.

Do-Ahead Virginia Smithfield Ham, Turkey & Stuffing

This recipe was served at an elegant restaurant in Richmond. After you discover the source for Smithfield ham, the rest is a breeze. I buy the turkey breast in the deli section. There's no fuss in serving since one serving per person is sufficient and the clean-up is a snap. Church members would often treat us to dinner in wonderful places "beyond our budget" like the restaurant that served this recipe. What grand memories we made! As a pastor's family we enter into so many people's lives, but the best part is that they enter our lives and widen our circle of friends. Like having children gets one "out of oneself," having a flock to tend does the same.

One 6-ounce box cornbread stuffing
One thin slice Smithfield ham per person
One thin slice turkey breast per person
One jar prepared turkey gravy

Prepare cornbread stuffing according to directions on package; set aside. In shallow glass casserole, arrange one slice Smithfield ham. With ice cream scoop, top with mound of dressing. Place slice of turkey breast on stuffing. Cover with foil and refrigerate. About 45 minutes before serving, remove from refrigerator to reach room temperature. Still covered, place in 350° oven for 10 minutes or until heated through. Open jar of turkey gravy, heat in microwave. Serve individual servings with hot gravy to ladle or pour.

Grandma Kikie's Apple Stuffed Pork Chops

Six 2-inch thick pork chops, with slit for pocket
1 small onion, finely chopped
2 ribs celery, finely chopped
½ loaf sandwich bread, torn in pieces and dried
2 Granny Smith apples, peeled and chopped
½ teaspoon rubbed dried sage
Salt and pepper
All-purpose flour
Hot water or canned chicken broth

Wash pork chops and pat dry with paper towel; set aside. Sauté onion and celery in vegetable oil until clear; transfer to a bowl and combine with next 4 ingredients. Mix well. Add enough hot water or broth to make stuffing moist. Stuff each pork chop pocket. Tip: Sometimes tiny skewers and twine are necessary to hold opening together. Mix flour, salt and pepper together and dredge chops in flour mixture. In cast iron or regular skillet, bring vegetable oil to medium high heat and sear both sides of pork chops to seal in juices. Transfer to a roaster and lay in single layer. With hot water, raise drippings in skillet and pour over chops. Place enough hot water to about cover the chops; cover and bake at 350° for 1½ to 2 hours. Check every 30 minutes or so to make sure they are not baking dry. Serves 6.

Little did my mother or I realize this entrée would be placed in the annals of history. While living in Columbia, Bill was a member of a think-tank group that included Rev. George Meetze, for years Chaplain of the South Carolina Senate. Dinner sites for meetings would be at members' homes, so in the late 1980's at our home, mother's menu of these pork chops, Waldorf salad and scalloped potatoes was served. Rev. Meetze thought it so tasty that he requested permission to publish and place it in the Caroliniana Library in Columbia, SC. To us, it was just homecookin'.

Modern-Day Appliances Meal

aige Parsons says, "This is a 13-minute gourmet dinner good enough for company or the Meat & Potatoes group." As a busy mother of 3 children, an active church member at Shandon Presbyterian Church, an auditing specialist for the State Treasurer of South Carolina, Paige makes every second of life count! While at Shandon in a singles group we started, Paige Hamilton met Cliff Parsons. Bill married them in 1980 and baptized 2 of their 3 children. Their love and support over these years have been a buoy in this "sea" called "life."

1 teriyaki pre-marinated pork tenderloin
8 to 10 new red potatoes, scrubbed but unpeeled
Water
One 16-ounce bag frozen crinkle-cut carrots
4 teaspoons margarine
¼ red onion chopped or onion salt to taste
1 tablespoon lemon juice
2 teaspoons honey
⅛ teaspoon cinnamon
⅛ teaspoon salt (omit if using onion salt above)

Using Indoor Grill, preheat indoor grill 5 minutes. Slice tenderloin lengthwise, not cutting all the way through, but so it can be "opened up" on the indoor grill, cut side down. Grill 8 minutes or until meat is cooked.

Using a Crockpot, place potatoes and enough water to generously cover potatoes in crockpot. Turn on low heat and cook for 8 hours.

Using a Microwave, prepare carrots according to package directions; drain and toss with sauce below.

Using the Stove, combine margarine, onion, lemon juice, honey, cinnamon, and salt in a saucepan. Cook until onions are tender. Toss with steamed carrots. Meal serves 4 to 5.

Boerenkool met Worst
(Kale, or farmer's cabbage, with sausage)

2 to 3 pounds fresh, curly kale or broccoli
3 pounds white potatoes, peeled and chunked
⅓ cup whole milk or half & half
Salt and pepper
4 tablespoons or more real butter
2 medium onions, chopped
Small amount vegetable oil
1 pound smoked sausage, knockworst or
big beef weiners

In 1995, our pathway in life led us to Market Square Presbyterian Church in Harrisburg. Church members, a tall Dutchman and chocolatier, Pieter Kooistra, and Margee shared their lives, their home, their thoughtfulness with many folks, especially the Arthurs, making our time there unforgettable. Lovely get-togethers by their restful lily pond, sharing good conversation with a variety of fascinating folks, provided respites for us both.

Strip, wash and cut up kale very fine and boil in a little water with a pinch of salt for about 20 minutes. In separate pot cook the potatoes in water. Drain water and add milk, salt and pepper and butter to potatoes. In small skillet sauté chopped onions in oil and add to potatoes. Combine cooked vegetables in a casserole. Adjust seasonings. Place pieces of cooked sausage, knockworst or weiners on top. Heat through in 350° oven for 20 minutes or microwave on high for 5 to 8 minutes. Serve with hearty bread, spread with mustard and for a salad, use applesauce. This is a typical Dutch winter dish. They believe in not cutting the kale "until the first frost has got it."

The Queen's Crown Pork Roast

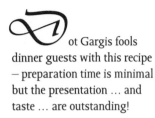

ot Gargis fools dinner guests with this recipe – preparation time is minimal but the presentation … and taste … are outstanding!

1 chicken bouillon cube
¾ cup boiling water
One 8-ounce package herbed season stuffing
1 tablespoon grated lemon rind
¼ cup finely chopped onion
½ teaspoon salt
3 tablespoons fresh or 1 tablespoon dried parsley
½ cup melted butter
2 tablespoon freshly squeezed lemon juice
One 14 rib crown pork roast
¼ cup sauterne

Make liquid chicken bouillon by using one cube and ¾ cup boiling water. In a bowl combine next 7 ingredients, add liquid bouillon. Stuff center of crown roast with mixture. Bake at 350° uncovered for 1 hour, basting with sauterne; cover and bake for additional 1 to 1½ hours, continue basting with sauterne. Serves 8 to 10.

Veal Scallopini

2 eggs
3 tablespoons milk
1 cup seasoned Italian bread crumbs
2 tablespoons flour
1 stick margarine
8 thin veal cutlets or thinly sliced pieces of veal
4 tablespoons white wine
2 onions, thinly sliced
1 green pepper, thinly sliced
8 ounces sliced fresh mushrooms

Lois Vaccaro, wife of Bill's first cousin Art, introduced me to this quick and easy entrée. Her own mother or her mother-in-law, Margaret Arthur Vaccaro, may have passed it on to her. Since the meat is very thin, "a little goes a long way."

In flat dish, beat egg with fork and stir in milk. In a second flat dish mix bread crumbs and flour together. Heat margarine in skillet. Rinse veal cutlets or pieces; dry with paper towel. Dip in egg wash, then in crumb mixture. Add to skillet and brown on both sides; remove and keep warm. Add white wine to "raise" browning mixture and to tenderize meat. Add onions, peppers and mushrooms and sauté a few minutes. Return veal to skillet; cover and simmer until done, generally about 25 to 30 minutes. Serve over cooked pasta. Serves 6.

Thin slices of pork tenderloin may be used if veal is difficult to find in meat market.

*Burrito Bake*:
1991 UGA Mother's Day Winner

To Ed Lunsford's amazement, his entry for "Favorite Recipe of Your Mom's" won first place. It was prepared for 4,000 UGA students and a printout of the quantities sent to Jackie Lunsford. In case you want to make it for 4,000 "friends," here's what you'll need: 583 pounds refried beans; 9 gallons of water; 164 pounds biscuit mix; 583 pounds of ground beef; 45 pounds of taco seasoning mix; 36 gallons picante sauce; 218 pounds Cheddar cheese and 72 pounds Monterey Jack cheese…and …166 pans. Good luck!!

1 pound ground beef, cooked and drained
One 1.25 ounce packet Taco seasoning
Butter or cooking oil spray
1 cup biscuit mix
¼ cup water
One 16-ounce can refried beans
1 cup thick salsa or picante sauce
1½ cups shredded mixed Cheddar and
Monterey Jack cheese
Sour cream, optional
1 avocado, sliced or guacamole, optional

In skillet brown ground beef, add Taco seasoning and continue cooking as directed until meat is cooked. Set aside. Butter or spray one deep 9- or 10-inch glass pie pan. Combine biscuit mix, water and refried beans. Make "crust" in pie pan. Layer beef, salsa, then cheese. Bake at 375° for 30 minutes. Serve with sour cream and/or avocado slices or guacamole. Serves 6 to 8.

E-Z Crockpot Mexican Stew

3 to 4 pounds stew beef or shish kebob pieces
Two to three 14.9-ounce cans whole kernel corn,
drained
1 cup salsa
1 cup barbeque sauce
One 1.25-ounce package Taco seasoning
One 19-ounce can garbanzo beans or chick peas,
drained
One 15-ounce can black beans, rinsed
1 bunch or less fresh cilantro, cut up

Put first 5 ingredients in crockpot. Cook on low heat for at least 8 hours. Remove lid and add garbanzo and black beans and sprinkle with cilantro. Replace lid and continue cooking until all ingredients are heated through. Serve over white rice or noodles. Serves 8 to 10 and keeps about a week in the refrigerator.

Another P.E.O. sorority sister, Carolyn Gilbert, who's busier in retirement than when she was in the school system, enjoys making this easy "fix and forget" stew for supper guests and family or to take as a "meal on wheels" for a new neighbor, someone sick or a shut in. Wouldn't you like to see her knock at your door with dinner?

Zucchini Beef Pie

Muriel and Tom Barbour and their two children lived two doors down from us in Richmond and were extended family to our children. When I fix this pie, I recall our neighborhood on West Club Lane — the very best place we could have raised our children during their most formative years. Our family faith and values were reinforced, support was understood, and horizons expanded by those neighbors.

1 pound ground beef
½ cup chopped green pepper
1 teaspoon dried parsley
1 teaspoon oregano
1 teaspoon salt
½ teaspoon dehydrated minced onion
½ teaspoon garlic salt
½ cup dry bread crumbs, divided
½ cup grated Parmesan cheese, divided
Two 9-inch pastry crusts
2 medium zucchini, sliced and divided
2 peeled tomatoes, sliced
1 tablespoon vegetable oil, divided
Milk
Salt and pepper

Brown ground beef; add green pepper and seasonings and sauté until green pepper is partially cooked. In a bowl mix together bread crumbs and Parmesan cheese. Grease and flour 9-inch pie plate; line with one crust. Layer one portion zucchini, one portion meat mixture, one portion crumb and cheese mixture; then add layer of one sliced tomato. Drizzle with half of oil. Repeat layers. Cut a few slits in second crust and place on layers, pinching edges together to seal. Brush top crust with milk and sprinkle with salt and pepper. Bake at 350° for 1 hour. Serves 6 to 8.

Spaghetti Pie

One 1-pound package sausage or Italian sausage,
cooked and drained
One 6 to 8-ounce box spaghetti, cooked,
drained and cooled
2 eggs, beaten
¾ cup grated Romano cheese
2 tablespoons butter
One 16-ounce container small-curd cottage cheese
or Ricotta cheese
One 16-ounce prepared extra thick spaghetti sauce
One 8-ounce package shredded Mozzarella cheese
Parmesan cheese

In large bowl mix eggs, Romano cheese and butter. Stir
together and add spaghetti, tossing to coat strands. Butter
one 10-inch glass pie plate and make "crust" with spaghetti
mixture. Put layer of cottage or Ricotta cheese; then a layer of
spaghetti sauce; then add layer of sausage. Bake 350° for 30
minutes. Remove from oven; add Mozzarella cheese and
return to oven a few minutes to melt cheese. Sprinkle with
Parmesan before serving. Serve with toasted garlic Italian
bread and tossed salad. Serves 6 to 8.

*Note: This pie freezes well. Thaw and bake as directed. For
years I served this to our junior high and senior high fellowship groups. A "neat and tidy" way to serve spaghetti!*

Guilarmo Arturo Spaghetti Sauce Italia

*T*he translated title means Bill Arthur's Italian Spaghetti Sauce! Ahhhh!

1 large onion, finely chopped
1 green pepper, finely chopped
⅓ cup finely chopped carrot
¼ cup finely chopped celery
4 to 6 tablespoons minced garlic
⅛ cup dried oregano
⅛ cup dried basil
Salt and pepper to taste
¼ cup balsamic vinegar
Two 28-ounce cans tomato puree
One 28-ounce can tomato sauce
One 12-ounce can tomato paste
One 14.5-ounce can chicken broth
1½ cups water
One 2-ounce link Italian sausage, mild,
cut in 1-inch pieces
One 2-ounce link Italian sausage, hot,
cut in 1-inch pieces

Sauté vegetables in a large pot in olive oil over medium heat for 10 minutes, stirring frequently. As vegetables begin to soften, add the garlic, oregano, basil, salt and pepper and balsamic vinegar. Add tomato puree, sauce, paste, chicken broth and water and cook at low-boiling simmer for approximately two hours, stirring often to avoid sticking. For added zest, drop 2 Italian sausage links — hot or mild - or both! — into the sauce. Be sure they are in the sauce long enough to be well cooked. It's recommended that they be added for the full second hour of cooking. Makes 3 quarts after cooking down.

Guilarmo Arturo's Meatballs Italia

These meatballs freeze well and if frozen in family-size servings, can be pulled out and ready for dinner in 30 minutes. Just spend some time one day making sauce and meatballs, and you'll have several meals prepared. Try a meatball sandwich on a hoagie bun. Could you translate this title?

2 to 3 tablespoons vegetable or olive oil
1½ cups finely chopped onion
2 eggs
2 links hot Italian sausage
2 links mild Italian sausage
2 pounds ground beef
¼ cup Italian bread crumbs
½ cup grated Parmesan cheese
1 teaspoon salt
½ teaspoon pepper
Spaghetti sauce

Heat oil in skillet and sauté onion until transparent. Set aside to cool. On wax paper squeeze sausages out of casing. In large bowl beat eggs and add both meats, cooked onions, and remaining ingredients. Mix thoroughly with hands or spoon, adding spaghetti sauce to hold mixture together. Shape into meatballs. Heat vegetable oil over medium low heat and drop in meatballs. Keep shaking the skillet on the burner to retain round meatballs. Brown meatballs for 15 to 20 minutes but do not make crisp. Cover bottom of long, flat glass casserole with spaghetti sauce. With slotted spoon, transfer meatballs in single layer to the casserole dish. Pour more spaghetti sauce over meatballs, cover with foil and bake in preheated 350° oven for 1 hour. Quantity of meatballs depend on size.

Veggie Manicotti

3 to 4 tablespoons olive oil
One 10-ounce box chopped spinach, cooked,
drained and squeezed dry
2 yellow squashes, sliced
1 red pepper, chopped
1 green pepper, chopped
1 medium onion, chopped
2 tomatoes, chopped
One 8-ounce package chopped fresh mushrooms
Other vegetables of your choice
Salt and pepper
½ teaspoon garlic powder or to taste
1 teaspoon dried oregano or to taste
One 16-ounce container Ricotta cheese
3 to 4 tablespoons Parmesan cheese
One 10-ounce jar spaghetti sauce
One 8-ounce package manicotti shells,
cooked al dente
One 8-ounce package shredded Mozzarella

*T*his is a rather economical dish, especially if you grow your own vegetables and make your own sauce. The same filling may be used with large shells instead of the manicotti tubes.

Tip: The vegetables may be prepared a day ahead and refrigerated.

In skillet heat olive oil and add prepared vegetables; season with salt and pepper, garlic powder, and oregano. Sauté until almost done. Combine all vegetables; add both cheeses. Mix well. In large flat casserole, pour enough spaghetti sauce to cover bottom. Stuff individual shells with veggie-cheese mixture and lay single layer in casserole. Cover with remaining spaghetti sauce and top with Mozzarella cheese. Bake at 350° about 45 to 50 minutes. Serve with Italian bread or garlic bread and tossed salad. Serves 4 or 5.

Baked Catch-of-the Day

2 pounds fresh orange roughy, tilapia or flounder
¾ cup all-purpose flour
1 tablespoon herbs de Provence *
3 tablespoons olive oil
3 tablespoons butter, cut in pieces
2 tablespoons fresh or frozen lemon juice
¼ to ½ cup dry white wine

Rinse fish and pat dry with paper towel. In long flat dish, mix flour and herbs. Dredge fish in flour mixture. In non-stick skillet heat olive oil and butter. Over medium heat, lightly brown fish on both sides. Transfer to a long, flat casserole in single layer. Drizzle lemon juice over fish and pour wine around pieces of fish. Bake uncovered in 350° oven for 25 to 30 minutes. Serve over rice pilaf — rice to which has been added currants and butter sautéed pignolia (pine) nuts. Serves 4.

Note: Personal preference is Georges Duboeuf Cuvee white table wine.

*Make your own Provence herbs by combining 3 tablespoons dried parsley, 3 tablespoons dried basil, 1 teaspoon rosemary, ½ teaspoon dried fennel seed, and 1 teaspoon thyme. Make several recipes and store in airtight container.

Stuffed Lemon Fish

4 pieces of talapia fish, filleted thin
2 packages frozen deviled crabs or 2 crabs each,
thawed
1 pound imitation crab
3 lemons, sliced thinly
½ to ¾ cup white wine
Butter
Soft bread crumbs, finely rolled
1 pound of fresh spinach
3 tablespoons olive oil

Wash fish and pat dry. In bowl mix together the deviled crab mixture and imitation crab. Divide evenly on the talapia fillets; roll up and place seam side down in glass casserole. Place sliced lemons over the fish rolls. Add white wine around fish and place pat of butter on each fish roll; sprinkle with bread crumbs. Bake at 350° for 30 to 40 minutes. While fish is baking, sauté fresh spinach in olive oil and set aside. When fish has baked for 30 to 40 minutes, remove from oven and top with sautéed spinach. Return to oven and bake an additional 10 minutes. Serves 4.

Crab Cakes

Two 8-ounce cans fresh backfin or claw crabmeat
½ teaspoon celery seed
½ teaspoon instant minced onion
½ teaspoon parsley
½ teaspoon black pepper
1 teaspoon Worcestershire sauce
1 teaspoon all-purpose mustard
3 tablespoons butter
3 to 4 tablespoons flour
½ cup milk
1 egg, beaten with fork
1 to 2 tablespoons milk
Cracker meal
Vegetable oil for frying

At various gatherings at Market Square Presbyterian Church in Harrisburg, we were told about how fantastic Nancy Motter's crab cakes were …. we tried them and are still concurring!

Note: These cakes may be made early in the day, loosely covered and refrigerated.

In bowl pick crabmeat for cartilage and shell pieces. Add celery seed, minced onion, parsley, black pepper, Worcestershire sauce and mustard; mix together and set aside. Melt butter; with whisk, stir in flour 'till smooth; add milk gradually, whisking to prevent lumps. Cook over medium heat, stirring constantly, until mixture leaves the side of the pan and forms a soft ball. Add more flour if necessary. Combine with crabmeat mixture; shape into cakes or patties. For egg wash, mix together egg and 1 to 2 tablespoons milk. Place dry cracker meal in separate flat container. Dip each crab cake in egg wash then into dry cracker meal. About 20 minutes before serving, in skillet heat oil over medium high heat and add crab cakes, frying 10 minutes for each side or until desired brown. Serve with cole slaw and stewed tomatoes. Serves 6.

Shrimp Bayou

This recipe was shared with us by Ginny Mickish, a member and delightful new friend at Eastminster Presbyterian Church in Stone Mountain, where Bill is doing yet another intentional interim pastorate. She served it as a first course, but it would make a marvelous cold-plate luncheon entrée.

2 pounds large shrimp
⅔ cup finely chopped celery
¼ cup thinly sliced green onion
1 tablespoon finely chopped parsley
1 cup vegetable oil
½ cup bottled chili sauce
3 tablespoons lemon juice
2 tablespoons horseradish
1 tablespoon prepared mustard
½ teaspoon paprika
½ teaspoon salt
Dash of Tabasco sauce
Shredded head lettuce

Heat a large pot of water to a rapid boil. Place shrimp in pot and cook exactly 3 minutes. Drain shrimp in colander and cool with cold water. Shell shrimp and devein. Put shrimp in a large bowl and add celery, onions and parsley. Combine remaining ingredients and pour over shrimp; mix gently. Cover securely, and refrigerate 12 hours before serving. Serve over a small amount of shredded lettuce. Serves 4 as an entrée or 8 for first course.

Hot Seafood & Cashews Casserole

2 pounds medium shrimp, shelled and deveined
Two 8-ounce cans crabmeat
2 tablespoons lemon juice
1 cup mayonnaise
1 small onion, grated
1½ cups finely chopped celery
One 6-ounce package cashew nuts, toasted
1½ cups New York sharp Cheddar cheese
One 2-ounce package potato chips
6 to 8 slivers of real butter

Rubye Philson featured this divine casserole on one of our visits to their Hilton Head condo in the mid-1980's. Peeling the shrimp is the most labor-intense part — but let your family or guests help and visit while peeling!

Bring 2 quarts of water to boil and add shrimp; cook 3 minutes only. Drain. With fingers check crabmeat for cartilage or shell. In mixing bowl combine shrimp, crabmeat and the next 6 ingredients. Place in 1½ to 2-quart casserole. Top with crushed potato chips. Dot with butter slivers. Bake 400° for 20 minutes only. Do not overcook as it toughens shrimp. A delectable menu to accompany this casserole is marinated cucumbers and onions, or a jelled avocado-cucumber salad, and stewed tomatoes. Serves 4 to 6.

Summer Breeze Shrimp & Pasta

*T*his is a light, cold, refreshing summer entrée for a luncheon or a dinner. Serve with fresh tomato slices, crisp cooked fresh asparagus and buttery round crackers. We have even taken this food in a cooler to Atlanta's Chastain Park for wonderful outdoor concerts.

1 pound large shrimp, shelled, cooked
and cut into chunks
1 hard-boiled egg, chopped
One 16-ounce box small shell pasta,
cooked and drained
½ teaspoon celery salt
2 teaspoons curry
One large bottle 1000 Island dressing
Salt and pepper

In large bowl combine shrimp, egg and pasta. Sprinkle with celery salt and curry. Stir in enough dressing to coat everything and make moist but not soupy. Add salt and pepper to taste. Keep refrigerated until time to serve. Serves 12. Don't let the curry scare you away from this mouthwatering salad!

Tip: To keep hard-boiled eggs from getting a black ring around the yolk, place in saucepan and cover with cold water 1-inch over top of eggs. Bring to full boil; turn off heat and let set for 17 minutes. Drain and cover with cold water.

Codfish à là Vizcaina

1 pound dried, salted codfish fillets
½ cup tomato sauce
½ cup olive oil
One 4-ounce jar chopped pimientos
¼ cup pimiento stuffed green olives
1 tablespoon capers
½ cup raisins
2 cloves garlic, peeled and crushed
1 bay leaf
2 hard-boiled eggs, cut in thin slices
1 pound potatoes, peeled and cut in small chunks
2 medium onions, peeled and thinly sliced

Cover codfish with water and soak at least 4 hours. Drain well and boil rapidly in 2 quarts fresh water for 15 minutes. Drain; discard skin and bones and shred fish with fork. Set aside. In a bowl mix together next 9 ingredients. Set aside. In a large non-stick frying pan arrange alternate layers of codfish, sliced potatoes, onions and tomato sauce mixture. Bring to a boil; cover; cook over low heat for 30 minutes or until potatoes are fork tender. Serves 6 to 8.

In October 1987, following a meeting in San Juan, Puerto Rico, we were hosted by a Presbyterian pastor and colleague, Manuel Jesus Perez-Rodriguez, and his wife Mercedes in Las Marias, the jungle, central part of Puerto Rico. Our last day there, we four were invited to a church family's home for a typical Puerto Rican country farm dinner, featuring this codfish entrée. For entertainment since conversing was difficult, the men visited in the living room while we three women toured the farm. Mrs. Vizcaina, armed with her machete, would often stop, whack a fruit from a tree, deftly whack it in half and we'd sip the juice as we continued. I asked to taste a fresh coffee bean — I seemed to "fly" back to the farmhouse where I announced, "Juanita Valdez has arrived!" To this day, I have never forgiven Bill for declining this adventure. What a memory!!

Traditional Christmas Eve Baccala

(Italian Codfish Stew)

The Christmas Eve tradition of eating fish, especially cod, as part of their religious observance of Christmas occurs many places around the world. This stew, combining fish and vegetables, is a simple but hearty one-dish meal, before the bounteous Christmas Day feast.

1 pound salted codfish, soaked,
allowing ¼ pound per person
3 tablespoons olive oil
4 to 5 red potatoes, quartered or sliced thickly
2 to 3 medium onions, quartered or sliced thickly
2 to 3 carrots, sliced into 1-inch pieces
One 11-ounce jar sun-dried tomatoes in oil,
cut up, divided
5 cloves garlic, minced
1 to 2 tablespoons dried oregano
2 tablespoons parsley, fresh or dried
Salt and pepper
½ to 1 cup water

At least 1 day before serving, cover codfish with water. Change water about 4 times during a 24-hour period to remove excessive salt. In 2½-quart deep casserole, pour olive oil to cover bottom. Layer red potato pieces, onion pieces, carrot slices and ¾ jar sun-dried tomato pieces. Sprinkle with garlic, oregano, parsley, small amount of salt-remember codfish is salted-and pepper. Cut up drained codfish into pieces and lay on top. Pour water around edges of casserole dish. Over cod pour remaining sun-dried tomato pieces and oil. Cover with aluminum foil and bake 350° for 1½ hours. Halfway through baking, gently stir stew. Serves 4. Serve with Italian or French bread, applesauce and white wine.

Breads

Azalia

Almond Poppy Seed Bread

An instructor in the Curriculum & Teaching department at Auburn University shared this recipe with me. It makes such a nice hostess, teacher or holiday gift.

3 cups all-purpose flour
2½ cups sugar
1½ teaspoons baking powder
1½ teaspoons salt
3 teaspoons poppy seeds
3 eggs, slightly beaten
1½ cups milk
1½ cups vegetable oil
3 teaspoons vanilla extract
3 teaspoons almond extract
3 teaspoons butter extracts
Sliced almonds for top of loaves

Mix first 5 ingredients. In a separate bowl mix eggs, milk, oil and extracts. Add liquid mixture to dry ingredients and beat 2 minutes. Spray 5 tinfoil mini-loaf pans or three 8" x 4" loaf pans with cooking oil spray. Pour batter evenly into pans. Sprinkle tops with almonds. Bake in 350° oven for 50 minutes to 1 hour, depending on size of pans. Remove from oven and cool slightly. While still warm, though, pour glaze over loaves. Freezes well.

Glaze:

¼ cup orange juice
¾ cup sugar
½ teaspoon vanilla
½ teaspoon almond
½ teaspoon butter extracts

Blend all ingredients in saucepan and bring to boil; reduce heat and simmer for 5 minutes.

Dilly Bread

1 package active dry yeast
¼ cup lukewarm water
1 cup creamed small-curd cottage cheese,
heated to lukewarm
2 tablespoons sugar
2 tablespoons instant minced onion
1 tablespoon butter, melted
2 tablespoons dill seed
1 teaspoon salt
¼ teaspoon baking soda
1 egg, unbeaten
2¼ to 2½ cups all-purpose flour

In small dish soften yeast in lukewarm water. In mixing bowl combine yeast mixture with next 8 ingredients, than add flour gradually to form stiff dough. Using mixer beat well after each addition. Cover; let rise in warm place 'till double in volume about 1 hour. Stir down dough and turn into buttered deep 8-inch round glass casserole, 1½-quart to 2-quart size. Cover and let rise 30 to 40 minutes. Bake in preheated 350° oven for 40 to 50 minutes or until brown. Remove from glass dish and brush top with melted butter and sprinkle liberally with salt.

Since Bill's mother Mary was a "do-it-from-scratch" cook, this is one of the few shortcut bread recipes she would make. Her delicious, homemade potato bread was always used for loaves. Until she retired and moved to Washington, DC area then to Florida, Mary lived almost her entire life within one block in Fairchance, Pennsylvania, but that runs in the family — her great-grandfather lived in the same county for 96 years and knew about 21 presidents' inaugurations. A devoted wife and mother, daughter and granddaughter, she found time to "play" every day. Maybe that's why Bill says, "A day without a party, is a day wasted." Her bread hot from the oven is a "smell of home" to our family.

Grandma Mary's Pecan Rolls

One 16-ounce box hot roll mix
Butter, softened
1 cup brown sugar
1 tablespoon ground cinnamon
Light Karo syrup
Chopped pecans
Small amount of water
Brown sugar
Ground cinnamon
Chopped pecans

Prepare hot roll mix according to directions; let rise. Generously butter one 9-inch square glass pan. Pour in brown sugar; sprinkle with cinnamon; drizzle with Karo syrup; add chopped pecans. If necessary add water a few drops at a time to partially liquefy sugar. Roll out dough; spread generously with softened butter; sprinkle with brown sugar, cinnamon and pecans. Roll up and slice the dough into 9 equal pieces. Place in pan and bake at 375° for 15 to 20 minutes.

Broccoli or Spinach Cornbread

One-half 10-ounce box frozen chopped broccoli
or spinach
1 stick real butter
One 8½-ounce box cornbread mix
4 eggs
Minced onion to taste
6-ounce container small curd cottage cheese

Cook broccoli or spinach, drain well and squeeze dry. Set aside. In 9 x 12-inch baking dish or comparable iron skillet, melt butter. Set aside. In a bowl combine by mixing well the cornbread mix, eggs, onion, cottage cheese and squeezed-dry broccoli or spinach. Add melted butter and mix again. In same baking dish or iron skillet, pour batter and bake 35 to 40 minutes in preheated 350° oven. Quite delicious served with a variety of soups.

An ever faithful friend for 20 years, Jackie Lunsford, served Taco Soup and this yummy cornbread on a cold November day at Pointe Jacqueline on Lake Murray, near Columbia. As an Army officer's wife, Jackie learned how to entertain in grand style and always "rolls out the red carpet" for house-guests. From big welcoming hugs to flowers in the guest room and guest bath, to scrumptious meals on their boat, around their Italian handmade dining room table, or sitting on the porch watching the sun set on the lake, you feel special.

E-Z Corn Fritters

½ stick real butter
½ stick margarine
1¾ cups biscuit mix
One 15-ounce can cream-style corn
Butter or margarine

*T*hese fritters were always on the party table of one of my party-giving mentors in Columbia, Rubye Philson. See if you can stop with one fritter!

Preheat oven to 400°. Place butter and margarine in jelly roll pan and melt in hot oven. In bowl combine biscuit mix and corn. Mix thoroughly. Remove pan from oven and with two spoons, put spoonful of batter on hot butter. Return to oven and bake 20 minutes. Turn fritters and add more butter and margarine, if necessary. Return to oven and bake another 20 minutes. Remove and serve hot or at room temperature. These are delightful served with Lemon Curd or Christmas Jam [see After Thoughts section]. Good for party faire, breakfast, lunch or dinner!

Figgy Apple Bread

¼ cup butter, softened
1 cup firmly packed brown sugar
2 eggs
1 ½ cups cored, peeled and grated apple
1 cup chopped figs
1 ½ cups all-purpose flour, sifted
¼ cup oat bran or regular oats
1 teaspoon baking soda
¼ teaspoon salt
½ cup chopped walnuts

Thoroughly grease and flour 1 large loaf pan or two 13-ounce coffee cans. Cream together softened butter and sugar until light and fluffy. Blend in eggs, one at a time, stir in grated apple and figs. In separate bowl thoroughly mix flour, oats, soda and salt. Add dry ingredients to butter/sugar mixture and gently blend. Stir in walnuts. Pour batter into pan or coffee tins. Fill each coffee tin only half full. Bake at 350° for 45 minutes or until top is lightly browned but yields to touch.

Ruth Marley and I became friends when we both worked at The Salvation Army Territorial Headquarters in Atlanta. We became kindred spirits through our love for her native Pennsylvania, cooking, and West Virginia buckwheat cakes! She is multi-talented and is filled with information about birds, music, and books, to name just a few. Ruth loves to entertain and her guests always are amazed at her seemingly effortless ability to prepare food and to create a picture-perfect presentation.

Strawberry Bread

1 cup butter
1 ½ cups sugar
1 teaspoon pure vanilla extract
¼ teaspoon lemon extract
4 eggs
3 cups sifted all-purpose flour
1 teaspoon salt
1 teaspoon cream of tartar
½ teaspoon baking soda
1 cup strawberry jam
½ cup dairy sour cream
1 cup broken walnuts, optional

In mixing bowl cream first 4 ingredients 'till fluffy. Add eggs, one at a time, beating well after each addition. Set aside. Sift together the dry ingredients; set aside. In separate bowl combine jam and sour cream and add alternately with dry ingredients to creamed mixture, beating 'till well combined. Stir in nuts. Divide among five greased and floured 4½ x 2¾ x 2¼ - inch loaf pans. Bake at 350° for 50 to 55 minutes or 'till done when inserted toothpick comes out clean. Cool 10 minutes in pans; invert and cool completely on wire racks.

Tip: Use 5 or 6 empty soup cans and fill two-thirds full instead of the loaf pans. Then for teas or receptions, slice the bread and spread softened cream cheese between two slices. Those "sandwiches" may even be cut in half for a different shape on a platter with other party treats. For eye appeal and variety, mix textures and shapes as well as colors in food.

Sweet Thangs

Apple

An E-Z Make-Your-Own Ice Cream

Having lived in towns where a large variety of ice creams were unavailable and to keep cost low for entertaining large groups, Bill devised this method for a real tasty treat!

One ½ gallon of inexpensive vanilla ice cream
One 10-ounce box or 12 or 16-ounce package frozen strawberries, raspberries, peaches or blackberries

or

4 Snicker or toffee bars, cut or broken into pieces

or

1 stack of Oreo cookies, broken into pieces, not crumbs

Carefully open ice cream container and place ice cream in large bowl to soften until able to stir — do not soften completely. At the same time, thaw frozen berries. Peaches will need cut into pieces. Stir either the fruit or candy bars or cookie pieces into ice cream. Return to original ice cream container and refreeze. Folks will think you've hand churned this ice cream!

Peach Blossom Ice Cream

½ gallon inexpensive vanilla ice cream
2 tablespoons ground cinnamon

Soften ice cream until mixable. Add cinnamon and mix thoroughly. Refreeze. Serve with sugared fresh peaches.

Coffee Ice Cream Dessert

ot Gargis' Coffee Ice Cream Dessert became our Amy's favorite one!

2½ cups vanilla wafer crumbs, divided
2 sticks margarine, softened
3 cups Confectioner's sugar
3 ounces unsweetened chocolate, melted
1 teaspoon pure vanilla extract
3 egg whites, stiffly beaten
1 cup chopped pecans
½ gallon coffee ice cream, softened

Spread 2 cups crumbs in a 9 x 13-inch buttered cake pan. Combine margarine, Confectioner's sugar, chocolate and vanilla. Fold in beaten egg whites and nuts. Spread over crumbs. Spread ice cream, ½ cup crumbs and nuts on top. Freeze 'till firm. Drizzle chocolate syrup over dessert squares at serving time.

Tip: Egg whites whip lighter if the eggs are room temperature and a pinch of cream of tartar is added after starting to froth.

Washday Rainbow Dessert

1 pint whipping cream
3 tablespoons sugar
1 teaspoon vanilla
18 to 20 coconut macaroons, crumbled fine
1 cup chopped pecans
½ gallon raspberry sherbet
½ gallon pineapple sherbet
½ gallon lime sherbet

This is a marvelous, eye-catching dessert. For readers who aren't old enough to remember how each day of the week had a task - Monday you washed, Tuesday you ironed, and so on — my early married years was at the bridge between one specific day and do it when you can. Since my big freezer was downstairs where my laundry area was located, I achieved both tasks with fewer trips up and down stairs.

Place small mixing bowl and beaters in freezer to get extremely cold. Whip cream and add sugar and vanilla. Fold in crumbs and nuts. Spread one-half of the mixture in 9 x 13-inch cake pan. Place in freezer to harden; set out half gallon of raspberry sherbet to soften. Put other half of first mixture in refrigerator to stay cold. Go do a load of washing. Put laundry in dryer. Remove frozen bottom layer and spoon in softened raspberry sherbet, return to freezer and remove half gallon pineapple sherbet to soften. Go do a load of washing. Put laundry in dryer. Remove pan from freezer and spoon softened pineapple sherbet on top of raspberry layer; return to freezer and remove half gallon of lime sherbet. Go do a load of washing. Put laundry in dryer. Remove pan from freezer and spread on last half of crumb, whipped cream mixture. Cover so it won't dry out. Return to the freezer and forget until time to serve and hopefully your laundry will be finished!

Indian Pudding

1 quart whole milk, divided
⅓ cup Indian meal* or regular yellow corn meal
½ teaspoon salt
Pinch of baking soda
¼ cup granulated sugar
½ teaspoon ground ginger
½ teaspoon ground cinnamon
¼ cup butter
½ cup dark molasses

This allegedly is an authentic recipe used by Indians when our country was first settled. Bill was introduced to it while attending seminary in Boston, Massachusetts. It has become the dessert for our made-from-scratch Boston Baked Beans (see Side Item section), grilled knockwurst, cole slaw, Kosher dill pickles, black bread New England dinner. So tasty on a cold winter's night.

In microwave heat 3 cups of milk. In large saucepan place Indian meal or regular yellow corn meal. Gradually stir in hot milk. Cook over low heat, stirring constantly, until mixture comes to a boil. In a small bowl mix together salt, soda, sugar, ginger and cinnamon. Add to corn meal mixture, cooking over low heat, stirring constantly for 15 minutes. Add butter, remaining 1 cup milk and molasses. Bake uncovered in 1½-quart deep casserole in 325° oven for 1½ to 2 hours without stirring, until set. Serve hot with cream, whipped cream sprinkled with ground nutmeg, vanilla ice cream or Nutmeg Hard Sauce and hermits. Serves 6 to 8.

Indian meal is a special order item. Old New Englanders claim it's the best to make true Indian pudding and say Indian meal is "where kernel meets cob."

Nutmeg Hard Sauce

⅓ cup butter
1 cup Confectioner's sugar
1 teaspoon vanilla extract
½ teaspoon ground nutmeg

Cream butter 'till light and fluffy. Gradually beat in sugar.
Beat until very light and puffy. Beat in vanilla and nutmeg.
Place a small spoonful of sauce on each serving of pudding.

Winter Hermits

4 tablespoons butter, at room temperature

½ cup packed light brown sugar

1 egg

1 cup sifted cake flour

½ teaspoon baking powder

¼ teaspoon allspice

¼ teaspoon ground ginger

¼ teaspoon nutmeg

1 cup currants or chopped raisins

¼ cup chopped walnuts or almonds

With electric mixer cream butter and beat in brown sugar and egg. On a sheet of wax paper sift together the next 5 ingredients; add to butter mixture. Dust the currants with a little flour and fold in the batter. Fold in nuts and blend well. Drop by spoonfuls onto a lightly greased baking sheet and bake in 350° oven for about 10 minutes. Especially good with Indian Pudding!

Chocolate Fondue

ondue is back! Just as styles of ladies' shoes and men's ties or suit lapels repeat every 15 or 20 years, so do food "crazes". When fondue became "in" once again, having this 1980's Dot Gargis' recipe in my personal cookbook proved my point.

One ½-pound Hershey's milk chocolate bar
¾ cup whipping cream, unwhipped
1 teaspoon instant coffee granules
2 tablespoons orange liqueur
Dash of cinnamon

Melt chocolate in double boiler or microwave on low until melted, watching that it does not burn. Gradually add whipping cream, instant coffee granules, orange liqueur and cinnamon. For a fondue occasion, put chocolate mixture in fondue pot. Provide apple and banana chunks or slices, white grapes, fresh strawberries, pineapple chunks, or pound cake squares for dipping. Another delicious way to serve this fondue is over vanilla ice cream. Stores well in a jar. At serving time, heat. Yields about one pint.

E-Z Peach Deluxe

4 fresh freestone peaches
⅓ cup brown sugar
Orange sherbet

When we would travel to Dot Gargis' Hilton Head condo or later on to her beach house to spend a long weekend, she would "pull out of her hat" simple but yummy recipes like this one.

Pour boiling water over fresh peaches. Let stand for 3 minutes. Skin peaches and twist in half. Cut peaches in bite-size pieces and stir in desired amount of brown sugar. Let set until the peaches get juicy. Serve over scoops of orange sherbet. Serves 3 to 4.

Oranges in Wine

This is an icy cold, clear and refreshing dessert that was shared with me by Ellie Allen, an active member of Market Square Presbyterian Church in Harrisburg.

¾ cup sugar
1 cup water
1 cup red wine
2 whole cloves
One 1-inch stick of cinnamon
One 1-inch vanilla bean
4 lemon slices
6 large seedless oranges

Combine sugar and water in a saucepan; cook, stirring until sugar dissolves. Add next 5 ingredients. Bring mixture to a boil; reduce heat and simmer for 15 minutes. Strain. While mixture is cooking, peel oranges cutting off all the white membrane. Slice thinly and pour hot wine syrup over the orange slices. Refrigerate for at least 4 hours to chill thoroughly. Can be prepared a day or two before serving. At serving time, spoon into dessert dishes.

Garden of Eden Baked Apples

6 cooking apples
¼ cup brown sugar
3 tablespoons real butter, softened
2 tablespoons slivered almonds
2 tablespoons apricot preserves
⅛ teaspoon salt
¾ cup orange juice
½ cup sugar
1 teaspoon minute tapioca

Peel ½-inch strip around middle of each apple. Core apples. Mix together softened butter, brown sugar, slivered almonds, apricot preserves and salt. Place an apple in individual baked apple dishes or in large glass custard cups. Stuff apples with butter mixture. In a separate bowl mix together the orange juice, sugar and tapioca for basting and pour over apples. Place apples in 350° oven and bake for 45 minutes. Every 10 minutes, baste with sauce. You'll be tempted to have two!

South Carolina Peach Cobbler

A South Carolina "peach", Kathryn Key, treated us to this fresh cobbler during our days in Columbia. Both South Carolina and its neighbor state, Georgia, produce huge peach crops. Shoppers can generally find both states' peaches in markets.

2 deep-dish pie crusts
3 to 4 cups fresh peaches
½ to 1 cup sugar
Juice of 1 lemon

Hard sauce:

3 tablespoons brown sugar
¼ to ½ teaspoon ground cinnamon
½ stick real butter

Fit one prepared crust in 2-quart casserole with high sides. In separate bowl cut up or slice peaches; add sugar and lemon juice. Fill crust. Top with second prepared crust; cut slits to allow steam to escape. Bake at 375° for 35 minutes or until bubbly. To make hard sauce, mix together brown sugar and cinnamon; cut in butter with fork. Add dollop to pieces of hot cobbler.

Grandma Mary's Apple Dumplings, Pennsylvania Style

2 cups all-purpose flour

2 teaspoons baking powder

1 teaspoon salt

⅔ cup shortening

½ cup milk

9 small cooking apples, like Granny Smith apples

1 cup sugar

1 cup water

¾ to 1 teaspoon ground cinnamon

¼ to ½ teaspoon ground nutmeg

2 tablespoons butter

Red food coloring

Mix together flour, baking powder and salt. Cut in shortening and add milk. On lightly floured surface, roll out dough and cut into 9 squares. Peel apples and cut in half. Place two halves in dough square, bring sides up around apple and seal dough. Place in buttered 9-inch square glass baking dish. Repeat until all 9 apples are in dish. In a saucepan, combine next 5 ingredients. Boil until butter melts and add a drop or 2 of red food coloring. Pour over apples. Bake in 350° oven for 30 minutes or until a cake tester or toothpick easily inserts in apple from top of dumpling.

Note: Individual dumplings may be prepared in large glass custard cups.

"Healthy" Oatmeal Cake

The Oatmeal Cake just has to be healthy, don't you think? My mother and grand-mother taught me to bake before I was 10 years old and if memory serves me right, this was one of my earliest "most difficult" cakes — with frosting, too! In my early 20's, our minister's wife, Yvonne Bourner, and I would spend hours pouring over recipes she'd gleaned through her years as a pastor's wife. There's where my recipe book began to branch out.

1 cup regular oats
1 stick margarine
1½ cups boiling water
1 cup white sugar
1 cup brown sugar, packed
2 eggs
1½ cups all-purpose flour
1 teaspoon soda
1 teaspoon cinnamon
1 teaspoon salt

In heatproof bowl place oats and margarine. Cover with boiling water. Let stand for 20 minutes; add white and brown sugars, then eggs. Sift dry ingredients together onto wax paper, then add to first mixture; beat until smooth. Pour into greased and floured 9 x 13-inch cake pan. Bake in 350° oven for 35 minutes. Do not overbake. Cool and top with frosting below.

Frosting:

1 egg
½ cup white sugar
¼ cup evaporated milk
6 tablespoons margarine
½ cup chopped pecans
1 cup shredded coconut
½ teaspoon pure vanilla extract

In saucepan beat egg and sugar then add evaporated milk and margarine. Stir constantly and bring to a rolling boil. Add pecans and coconut; stir to mix. Add vanilla; mix again. Spread on top of cooled oatmeal cake.

Quick-as-a Wink Cake

One 1-pound box Angel Food cake mix
One 20-ounce can crushed pineapple, undrained
Whipped topping
Maraschino cherries

Fellow "book worm," Barbara Block, shared this recipe and a few other "quickies" with me one evening at a Book Club meeting.

Place cake mix in bowl adding only the crushed pineapple. Stir until all dry ingredients are moistened. Grease one 9 x 13-inch cake pan with vegetable spray. Pour in batter. Bake at 350° for 30 minutes. Remove from oven; cut into squares. Top with whipped topping and add a maraschino cherry. Oh yes, and don't forget to pat some flour on your nose to show how hard you've worked all day to make this cake!

Brown Sugar Pound Cake

Between a Christmas engagement and a mid-April wedding, Circle 2 at the First United Presbyterian Church in Clarksburg took me under their wings. Bill was the first pastor in the church's 150-year history to get married so everyone was "a-twit." This cake is just one recipe an active Circle member, Donna Smith, shared. We became kindred souls, especially in the cooking department.

3 sticks margarine, softened
2 cups packed brown sugar
1 cup white sugar
5 eggs
1 teaspoon pure vanilla extract
3 cups all-purpose flour
1 teaspoon baking powder
½ teaspoon salt
1 cup milk
1 cup chopped pecans

Cream together the margarine and sugars. Add eggs one at a time, beating well after each egg; add vanilla extract. On wax paper, sift together flour, baking powder and salt. Add flour mixture alternately to batter with 1 cup milk. Fold in chopped nuts. Transfer to a greased and floured tube pan. Bake in 350° oven for 1 hour 15 minutes. Do not open oven while cake is baking!

Peanut Butter 'n Chocolate Chip Cake

2¼ cups all-purpose flour

2 cups brown sugar, packed

1 cup smooth peanut butter

½ cup real butter, softened

1 teaspoon baking powder

½ teaspoon baking soda

1 cup milk

1 teaspoon pure vanilla extract

3 eggs

One 6-ounce package semi-sweet chocolate chips

One of our longest, steadfast, "adopted-family" friends from Clarksburg, my hometown and where we served the First Presbyterian Church, Lil Gordon, made this Peanut Butter Cake especially for the initial visit of our 2-year-old granddaughter in June 2000. Needless to say, Mary Elizabeth gobbled it up!

Combine in large bowl flour, brown sugar, peanut butter and butter. Blend 'till crumbly. Reserve 1 cup of mixture. Add to remaining crumb mixture in bowl the next 5 ingredients. Blend at low speed 'till ingredients are moistened, then beat 3 minutes at medium speed. Pour batter in a greased (bottom only) 9 x 13-inch pan and sprinkle with reserved 1 cup of crumb mixture. Sprinkle the chocolate chips over crumb mixture and place in 350° oven, baking for 35 to 40 minutes.

Summer Breeze Strawberry Cream Cheese Cake

Suzie Baur, another "bookworm" friend and active member of Eastminster Presbyterian Church in Marietta, shared this refreshing and luscious-looking recipe with me.

2 pints small to medium-size strawberries
One 8-ounce block cream cheese
½ cup sugar
¾ teaspoon pure vanilla extract
1 pint whipping cream
3 packages ladyfingers

About an hour before making, place small mixing bowl and beaters in freezer for whipping cream. Clean strawberries and slice in half. Whip together cream cheese, sugar and vanilla. Remove bowl from freezer and whip cream until stiff; fold into the cream cheese mixture. Using a springform pan place ladyfingers upright first around the side and then on the bottom of pan. Fill pan with half the cream mixture and press in half the strawberries. Add a layer of ladyfingers on top of this mixture. Pour the other half of the cream mixture on top of ladyfingers and then press in strawberries in a decorative pattern on top. Chill at least 2 to 3 hours. When ready to serve, place pan on serving plate and unmold sides of pan. Decorate with extra whole strawberries. Serves 8 to 10.

Black Forest Cheesecake

One 20-ounce package Oreo cookies
1 tablespoon butter, softened
1 pint small-curd cottage cheese
Two 8-ounce blocks cream cheese
1 ½ cups sugar
4 eggs
⅓ cup cornstarch
2 tablespoons lemon juice
1 teaspoon pure vanilla extract
½ cup butter, melted
1 pint sour cream
One 1-pound 5-ounce can cherry pie filling
1 can aerosol whipped cream

Mary Ann Saluga is Bill's first cousin. She hails from western Pennsylvania and has just retired as a high school teacher. She and her husband Paul visit us in Atlanta once each year and you guessed it, we ... even the men ... always talk recipes!

In food processor whir cookies until fine crumbs. Butter sides and bottom of springform pan and dust sides of pan with some cookie crumbs, then spread 1 cup of the crumbs on bottom of the pan. Cream cottage cheese and cream cheese until smooth. In mixing bowl mix sugar and eggs; add cheese mixture, blending well. With mixer on low add next 5 ingredients, mixing until smooth. Pour half the batter into prepared pan; sprinkle with 1 cup cookie crumbs. Dip out about half the cherry pie filling and carefully place at random on top of crumbs. Carefully pour remaining batter on top; sprinkle remaining crumbs over all. Bake at 325° for 1 hour 10 minutes. Turn oven off. Leave cheesecake in oven to cool for 2 hours. Do not disturb! Before serving decorate top with remaining cherry pie filling and dollops of aerosol whipped cream.

One-Bowl Blonde Brownies

While living in Richmond, we were invited to Hilda Foster's home for Christmas Eve to share their family dinner. With her "classy" British demeanor, Bill dubbed her "Lady Hilda."

2 cups all-purpose flour
1 teaspoon baking powder
¼ teaspoon baking soda
½ teaspoon salt
2 cups brown sugar, packed
1 cup chopped pecans
⅔ cup melted butter
2 eggs
One 6-ounce package chocolate chips

Mix together all dry ingredients. Add butter and eggs; stir in chocolate chips. Batter will be stiff. Press into greased and floured 9 x 13-inch cake pan. Bake in 350° oven for 20 minutes.

E Z Aloha Brownies with Variations

One 15½-ounce can crushed pineapple, undrained
One 5-ounce package flaked coconut, optional
One 1-pound, 2.25-ounce box yellow cake mix
1 stick real butter, solid
Whipped topping

A soul mate in cooking, Barbara Block, shared these quick ideas with me at a Book Club meeting one night. Using ingredients busy gals and guys can have on hand, make these yummy cake recipes invaluable. Children can even whip up these cakes!

Pour undrained pineapple in a 9 x 13-inch cake pan, making sure it's evenly distributed. Sprinkle coconut on top of fruit. Add dry cake mix, mashing with fork to get rid of lumps and distribute evenly. Thinly slice stick of butter placing squares so that the dry cake mix is completely covered. Bake at 350° for 45 minutes to one hour. When top is golden brown, remove from oven. Cool slightly. Cut into squares. Add dollop of whipped topping.

Variations:

Spray pan with cooking oil and distribute one 1-pound 5-ounce can cherry pie filling on bottom. Sprinkle with toasted chopped pecans. Add dry chocolate cake mix. Thinly slice stick of butter and arrange to cover dry mix. Bake as above.

Spray pan with cooking oil and distribute one 1-pound 5-ounce can blueberry pie filling on bottom. Sprinkle with toasted slivered almonds. Add dry lemon cake mix. Thinly slice stick of butter and arrange to cover dry mix. Bake as above.

Picnic Fruit Squares

Another cousin, Mary Ann, makes this recipe almost every year for the family reunion picnic.

1 cup butter or margarine
1½ cups granulated sugar
4 eggs, beaten
2 cups all-purpose flour
1 teaspoon vanilla extract
1 teaspoon lemon extract
One 1-pound 5-ounce can cherry pie filling
Confectioner's sugar

In a large mixing bowl cream together the butter and sugar. Add the eggs and flour. Mix in the extracts; blend well. Spread the batter into a greased 15½ x 10½ x 1-inch pan. Cut the surface of the batter to make 28 squares. Spoon the pie filling in the center of each square. During baking, the batter puffs up around the pie filling. Bake in a 350° oven for 45 minutes or until golden brown. Cut into squares. Cool completely in pan. Sprinkle with Confectioner's sugar. Remove from pan.

Note: Other fruit pie fillings may be used, such as blueberry, pineapple or apple.

Glazed Fresh Blueberry Pie

One 9-inch pastry crust, baked and cooled
One 3-ounce package cream cheese, softened
4 cups fresh blueberries, divided
¾ cup sugar
3 level tablespoons cornstarch
½ cup water
2 tablespoons lemon juice

Spread entire inside of baked, cooled crust with cream cheese. Place 3 cups washed and paper-towel-dried fresh blueberries in crust. Force the sugar and cornstarch through a medium-size sieve over a bowl; set aside. In small saucepan place 1 cup fresh blueberries and water. Bring just to boil; reduce heat, and simmer 2 minutes. In a small bowl strain cooked berries by forcing through small sieve with spoon. Scrape bottom of sieve and add to juice. Measure ½ cup juice and set aside. In same saucepan add the sugar/cornstarch mixture and gradually stir in juice. Cook over medium heat, stirring constantly, until mixture is thick and clear. Cool slightly; add lemon juice. Pour over berries in crust and with rubber spatula, work glaze through berries, leaving cream cheese in bottom undisturbed. Chill. Trim with pastry daisies or leave plain. Serve with whipped cream.

Frozen Peanut Butter Pie

4 ounces cream cheese, softened
1 cup Confectioner's sugar
⅓ cup extra crunchy peanut butter
½ cup milk
4 ounces frozen whipped topping, thawed
One 9-inch graham cracker crust

Beat cream cheese 'till fluffy. Beat in Confectioner's sugar and peanut butter. Add milk slowly, blending thoroughly with spoon. Fold in thawed whipped topping. Pour in crust. Freeze 'till firm, then cover. Cut while frozen.

Note: Sometimes the prepared crusts have a clear plastic cover. If not, freeze then cover with plastic wrap.

Another version using a different crust:

¾ cups peanut butter chips, chopped
1 cup vanilla wafer crumbs
5 tablespoons butter, melted

With rolling pin, crush vanilla wafers; set aside; chop chips in food processor and combine with vanilla wafer crumbs in pie pan. Drizzle with melted butter; press firmly and freeze. Ready to fill any time after frozen.

To-Die-For Southern Pecan Pie

After 25 years, this pecan pie recipe is my all-time favorite. Thanks to Joanne Sellers, a member of Shandon Presbyterian Church in Columbia, for sharing this recipe with me.

3 eggs
1 cup sugar
1 cup Karo dark syrup
2 tablespoons butter, melted
1 teaspoon pure vanilla extract
1 cup coarsely chopped pecans
One 9-inch unbaked pie crust

In mixing bowl beat eggs. Add sugar, syrup, butter, and vanilla. Mix well. Fold in nuts. Pour into crust. Bake at 400° oven for 15 minutes. Reduce heat to 325°; bake 30 additional minutes or 'till done. Note: Lay piece of foil over top if getting too dark. The center will shake a wee bit but will settle when cooled. Serve with whipped cream or vanilla ice cream.

Tip: Spray measuring cup with cooking oil before adding Karo syrup. It will pour out "clean as a whistle" as my dad used to say.

Bacon & Eggs Treat

Pretzel sticks
White chocolate bark
Yellow M&M candies

On paper plate, place 2 pretzel sticks (the "bacon") side by side. Cut about a ½" square chunk of the white chocolate bark (the "egg white") and place in middle of pretzel sticks. Microwave on high for about 1 minute, watching that it does not start to burn. Remove and press one yellow M&M (the "egg yolk") in center of white chocolate, then press pretzel sticks together to keep in tact when chocolate cools. Note: In order to make a large batch of these, start saving the yellow M&M's early or have friends help in your collection.

My granddaughter, Mary Elizabeth, and I made these one Saturday afternoon for a fun project. On Monday, her mommy had to take treats for the nursery school children who were learning "B/b" and "yellow" that week. They were a big hit! I look forward to us making them one day with her baby sister, Sarah Margaret. This recipe was shared with me by my co-worker Tracey Duren who's son's Ohio grandmother made them for him as a treat.

E-Z White Chocolate Chews

1 pound white chocolate chunks
1 cup lightly salted peanuts
1 cup coarsely chopped walnuts
1 cup coarsely chopped pecans
1 cup broken-in-half 2-inch pretzel sticks

In microwave watching carefully, melt white chocolate chunks. Stir in remaining ingredients and drop by teaspoonfuls on wax paper; let cool. These Chews can either be cookies or candy.

E-Z Cracker Candy

Round buttery crackers
Peanut butter
White or dark chocolate bark

Put 2 crackers together with peanut butter. In microwave or in double boiler, melt chocolate bar. Use enough bark or a small container to make the melted chocolate deep for dipping. Dip each cracker "sandwich" in melted chocolate; let set while holding, then place carefully on wax paper. If your fingers have left a mark, dip a toothpick in the chocolate and mend. These pieces are showy on a cookie platter or make marvelous homemade gifts. For Christmas, tint with red food coloring one part of the white chocolate; use green in a second part of white chocolate. Yellow food coloring is "Springy" around Easter time. Just think of what colors you could use for baby showers, July 4th celebrations. . .

Yule Log Yummies

At holiday time, I divide my white chocolate into thirds: one white, one tinted red, one tinted green. I do not use the milk or semi-sweet chocolate with that combination. These are also a different shape and texture for a cookie tray or on a plate at the bottom of a stemmed dish filled with ice cream. Thanks, Paige Parsons, for adding pizzazz to pretzels.

One 14-ounce package individually wrapped caramels
2 tablespoons milk
One package large log stick pretzels
1 cup chopped toasted pecans
One block white chocolate bark
One 12-ounce package milk or semi-sweet chocolate chips

Unwrap caramels and place in 2-cup glass measuring cup. Add milk and microwave until caramels are melted. Stir. Dip each pretzel log two-thirds of the length in the caramel mixture and roll in toasted pecans. Place on wax paper lined cookie sheet and refrigerate. Wait 1 hour. Melt white chocolate bark in small measuring cup with spout; remove logs from refrigerator and keep turning while drizzling with white chocolate. Return to refrigerator. Wait 1 hour. Melt milk or semi-sweet chocolate chips in a small measuring cup with spout. Remove logs from refrigerator and keep turning while drizzling with chocolate. Return to refrigerator. If house is cool, leave out. They tend to get soggy if left too long in refrigerator; that is, if they last that long!

E-Z Sugar-Cinnamon Tortilla Toasties

Butter-flavored cooking spray
Eight 6-inch flour tortillas
¼ cup granulated sugar
1 teaspoon ground cinnamon

A co-worker at The Salvation Army Territorial Headquarters, Mary Ann Cox, fixed these treats often for her grandchildren. They are fail proof and children enjoy helping.

Spray cookie sheet with sides with butter cooking spray. Cut tortillas in quarters or wedges. Place on cookie sheet. Spray with butter cooking spray. In a bowl mix together sugar and cinnamon and sprinkle liberally on wedges. Lightly spray again with butter cooking spray. Bake at 350° until toasted, usually 3 to 4 minutes. These treats are tasty with peaches and ice cream or just plain ice cream. Store in airtight container.

Dates to Remember

Pitted dates
Extra crunchy peanut butter
Granulated white sugar

Janet Birch and her husband David we've known through church circles for years. After about a 25-year separation, we were reunited in Harrisburg in 1995. When we had to be evacuated in mid-January 1996 from our home in Shipoke because of a flood, the Birches took our homeless souls into their warm and cozy home for several days. While there, Janet served these dates as "Christmas Leftovers." We "flew into them like white on rice", as my co-worker from Pascagoula, Mississippi used to say.

With table knife, open slit in each date and fill with peanut butter. Roll in granulated white sugar. Stack in container that seals and store in refrigerator. This is a delightful addition to a cookie tray or at the end of a meal or to serve as candy. Nutrition and fiber may be found in the date and peanut butter. This is rather time-consuming but can be done while sitting and chatting or watching television. Quantities depend on number desired.

E-Z No-Bake Bars for Kids of All Ages

Our daughter Amy and her friends make these quite often for their children's school and party treats.

4 cups Cheerios
2 cups crisp rice cereal
2 cups dry roasted peanuts
2 cups M&M candy
1 cup light corn syrup
1 cup sugar
1½ cups creamy peanut butter
1 teaspoon vanilla extract

In a large bowl combine cereals, peanuts and M&M's; set aside. In a saucepan bring corn syrup and sugar to a boil. Cook and stir just until sugar is dissolved. Remove from the heat; stir in peanut butter and vanilla extract. Pour over cereal mixture and toss to coat evenly. Spread into a greased 15 x 10 x 1-inch jellyroll pan. Press mixture into pan with waxed paper or oil-sprayed wooden spoon. Cool; cut into squares. Makes fifteen 3 x 3-inch squares or many more if cut smaller. Warning: Do not serve to small children under 3 years because of peanuts and candy.

Toffee Bars

Graham crackers
1 cup brown sugar
2 sticks real butter
12-ounce package semi-sweet chocolate chips
1 cup chopped pecans
Cooking oil spray

The Toffee Bars cut a "fine line" between cookies and candy, so use them interchangeably. A Shandon Presbyterian Church supper club and good friend from Columbia days, Kathy James, shared this recipe with me years ago.

Line 10 x 15-inch jellyroll pan with tin foil and spray with vegetable oil. Arrange one layer of graham crackers over foil. In saucepan cook the brown sugar and butter until foamy, making toffee mixture. Pour on graham crackers and bake in 350° oven for 12 minutes. Remove from oven and sprinkle immediately with chocolate chips. As they start melting, spread over entire surface of toffee mixture. Sprinkle with chopped pecans, pressing them into chocolate. Refrigerate until hard. Break into pieces.

Cheesecake Cookies

⅓ cup margarine, softened
⅓ cup brown sugar
1 cup flour
½ cup chopped pecans
One 8-ounce block cream cheese
¼ cup sugar
1 egg, slightly beaten
1 tablespoon lemon juice
2 tablespoons milk
1 teaspoon pure vanilla extract

Cream together margarine, brown sugar and flour. Set aside 1 cup of this mixture and press remaining mixture into 8-inch square pan and bake in 350° oven for 10 to 15 minutes. Remove from oven and set aside to cool. In a separate bowl cream together cream cheese and sugar. Add last 4 ingredients, beating until smooth. Spread on baked crust. Put 1 cup reserved topping on cream cheese layer. Bake at 350° for 25 minutes more. Store in refrigerator. This recipe may be doubled for a 9 x 13-inch pan.

The Arthur Family Christmas Cookies

The cookie dough takes 20 minutes to make but the cookies take all day to make! Since our children, Amy and David, were small, this has been a mother-children project. It was fascinating watching the reindeer finally have 4 legs, the snowmen … I guess they're called snow people now … with white icing only, or the angels without clipped wings as the children's dexterity and my patience improved with age. What memories!

1 cup real butter
1½ cups sugar
3 eggs
1 teaspoon pure vanilla extract
3½ cups all-purpose flour
2 teaspoons cream of tartar
1 teaspoon baking soda
½ teaspoon salt

Cream together butter and sugar. Add eggs one at a time. Stir in vanilla extract. On a sheet of wax paper, sift together the last 4 ingredients. Gradually add flour mixture to first mixture. Stir until thoroughly mixed. Refrigerate overnight in a tightly sealed container. When ready to roll out and cut, lightly flour a bread board. Roll out a small portion at a time to ⅜-inch thickness. Cut with cookie cutters and decorate. Place on ungreased cookie sheets. Bake at 375° for 6 to 8 minutes. Cool on sheet and remove to rack. Ice with a thin icing if desired. Yummy with milk for Santa!!

Thin icing can be made by pouring Confectioner's sugar in a bowl and gradually adding milk or water until desired consistency. A drop of vanilla, lemon or almond extract may be added for flavor. Add food coloring. If too runny, just add more Confectioner's sugar. Tip: A small bowl for each color of icing will be needed.

After Thoughts

Lilac

Lemon Curd

4 lemons
5 eggs
1 stick real butter, no substitution
2⅓ cups sugar

To transition the Arthurs from Richmond to Columbia in 1979, our dear friend, Hilda Foster, placed us in the hands of one of her longest friends from England, Olive Barnett. They had met in Richmond as members of a WWII English war brides group and became fast friends. Olive, like Hilda, shared with me so many English recipes like this Lemon Curd and were continual reminders of my ancestors from across "the pond."

Wash lemons and grate rind very finely. Cut lemons in half and squeeze out the juice. Set aside. Beat eggs, then put eggs, lemon rind and juice, butter and sugar into top of double boiler.* Stir until sugar is dissolved and mixture cooks and thickens. When it is thick, strain into small pre-warmed jars and cover immediately. Keep refrigerated. Serve on toasted English muffins, crumpets or Corn Fritters (See Bread section). I have even used it for filling between split cake layers. I leave some extra rind in the curd for texture but that alters the pure English curd.

I now use the microwave instead of a double boiler, watching that the egg mixture doesn't burn.

Pasta with Faux Beef Drippings

This is a wonderful alternative to potatoes or rice for a beef entrée.

3 to 4 garlic cloves, do not substitute
6 tablespoons butter, melted
3 sprigs or 5-inches fresh rosemary
1 teaspoon beef bouillon granules
2 to 3 servings pasta

Peel garlic and smash under flat side of knife blade. In skillet combine butter, garlic, rosemary and bouillon granules. Simmer over low heat until flavors are well blended. Set aside. Cook pasta (spaghetti or linguine or fettuccine or angel hair) and drain. Over drained pasta, strain butter mixture through sieve and toss. Additional melted butter may be required.

Do-Ahead Cranberry Chutney

One 12-ounce package fresh cranberries
1½ cups sugar
¾ cup water
⅓ cup orange juice
¾ cup golden raisins
¾ cup chopped walnuts
¾ cup chopped celery
1 small apple, chopped
1 tablespoon grated orange peel
1 teaspoon ground ginger

At least 2 days before serving, wash and pick through fresh cranberries removing dried stems and discarding shriveled berries. In saucepan heat berries, sugar and water to boiling point, stirring frequently. Reduce heat and simmer for 15 minutes. Remove from heat, stir in remaining ingredients. Cover and refrigerate. This chutney will keep refrigerated for 2 to 3 weeks and, is a marvelous accompaniment for poultry, ham, or pork entrées or sandwiches.

Christmas Jam

1 cup fresh cranberries
One 10-ounce package frozen strawberries, thawed
2 cups sugar

Wash cranberries, removing dried stems and discarding shriveled berries. Re-measure to make 1 cup. Pour cranberries in food processor and chop. In saucepan place chopped cranberries and strawberries, bringing to a boil. Add sugar and boil 'till thickened. Pour into jelly glasses. Seal with melted paraffin or just refrigerate. This jam may be served on biscuits, toasted English muffins, crumpets or Corn Fritters (See Bread section).

To use paraffin: With fingers bend one section of a small, metal coffee can to make pouring spout. Pour 1 to 2 inches of water in a pan. Place tin can in water; add 1 to 2 blocks of Gulfwax paraffin to can. Heat the water and simmer until paraffin melts. Pour on top of jam in jelly glasses. Be careful not to get hot wax on your skin. Let paraffin completely set, then screw on lids.

West Virginia Hot Dog Chili

1 pound ground beef, ground twice
1 clove garlic
1 large onion, chopped fine
1 tablespoon chili powder
1 tablespoon brown sugar
Two 8-ounce cans tomato sauce
Salt and pepper to taste
Pinch of hot pepper or dash of pepper sauce

Brown beef, garlic and onion together. Add remaining ingredients and cook 30 minutes. Serve on hot dogs. It freezes well.

Tip: If placed in small re-closable freezer bags and flattened, they stack to save freezer space and take less time to thaw.

Many West Virginias generally consider hot dogs inedible unless topped with chili. They are as peculiar and varied in their tastes regarding hot dog chili as Georgians are regarding barbecue and pecan pie. My choice recipe for hot dog chili was passed on to me from my mother who received it back in the 1950's from a cook at the Mt. Clare Elementary School in West Virginia.

After Thoughts

Christmas Jam, 157
Do-Ahead Cranberry Chutney, 156
Lemon Curd, 154
Pasta with Faux Beef Drippings, 155
West Virginia Hot D 158

Breads

Almond Poppy Seed Bread, 112
Broccoli or Spinach Cornbread, 115
Dilly Bread, 113
E-Z Corn Fritters, 116
Figgy Apple Bread, 117
Grandma Mary's Pecan Rolls, 114
Strawberry Nut Bread, 118

Breakfasts & Brunches

All Seasons French Toast, 23
Ambrosia of the Gods, 26
Anytime Cheesy Egg Bake, 28
Bravo Breakfast, 22
Early Marriage Goldenrod Eggs, 24
Eggs in Herb Tomato Sauce, 25
Frosty Morn Sausage Coffee Cake, 33
Hearty Hash Brown Omelet, 36
Hoppin' Red Bunny, 35
Indoor Grill Breakfast Apple Tortilla, 29
Maple Bacon Oven Omelet, 27
Meal-in-One Egg Casserole, 32
Melon Wrap, 26
Pap Pap's Pancakes, 30
Popular Cheese & Eggs with a Twist, 31
Skillet Almond Coffee Cake, 34

Entrées

Baked Catch-of-the-Day, 103
Boerenkool met Worst (Kale, or farmer's cabbage, with sausage), 93
Burrito Bake: 1991 UGA Mother's Day Winner, 96
Chicken & Cots, 84
Chicken Marsala with Mushrooms, 82
Codfish ala Vizcaina, 109

Crab Cakes, 105
Deviled Chicken, 86
Do-Ahead Virginia Smithfield Ham & Turkey with Stuffing, 90
E-Z Crockpot Mexican Stew, 97
E-Z Pot Poulet, 83
Grandma Kikie's Apple Stuffed Pork Chops, 91
Guilarmo Arturo Spaghetti Sauce Italia, 100
Guilarmo Arturo's Meatballs Italia, 101
Hot Seafood & Cashew Casserole, 107
Italian Chicken Breasts, 85
King Min's Crown Pork Roast, The, 94
Shrimp Bayou, 106Chicken, 87
Leftover Turkey Casserole, 89
Modern-Day Appliances Meal, 92
Queen's Crown Pork Roast, The, 94
Shrimp Bayou, 106
South-of-the-Border Chicken with Green Chilies, 88
Spaghetti Pie, 99
Stuffed Lemon Fish, 104
Summer Breeze Shrimp & Pasta, 108
Traditional Christmas Eve Baccala, 110
Veal Scallopini, 95
Veggie Manicottti, 102
Zucchini Pie, 98

Punches, Munchies & More

Always Ready Appetizers, 12
Amaretto Cheese, 13
Crescent Moon Baked Brie, 14
Deluxe Beef & Pecan Spread, 15
Fireside Hanover Pretzels, 20
Icy Mocha Coffee, 9
Jump Start Juice, 8
Mexican Roll-Ups, 16
Orange Pecans, 11
Pretend-to-be-Rich & Famous Appetizer, 17
Southern Muggy Day Pineapple Slush, 10
Spicy Pecans, 11
Sure-Winner Dip, 18
Vidalia Onion Dip, 19

Side Items

Amaretto Hot Fruit Compote, 72
Amy's Favorite – Orange Baked Beans, 60
Autumn Scottish Turnips & Apples, 71

Baked Fresh Asparagus, 62
Cabbage with Glazed Onions, 77
Caramelized Carrots, 62
Caramelized Vidalia Onions, 76
Corn Pudding, 70
E-Z Green Beans ala Dijon, 79
Elegant Rice Casserole, 64
Fresh Tomato Pie, 65
Garlic Grits Casserole, 61
Grandma Mary's Scalloped or Au gratin Potatoes, 67
Grandma VanHorn's E-Z Old-Fashioned Succotash, 66
Orange Beets, 68
Quick Butternut Squash, 69
Redskin Mashed Potatoes, 78
Showy Broccoli Sunburst, 73
Suth'rn Per'low, 74
Sweet Potato Fries, 75
Tailgating Marinated Broccoli, 63
Vidalias with a Kick, 77
Zucchini Fans for Non-Fans of Zucchini, 80

Soups, Salad & Sandwiches

Artichoke & Rice Salad, 51
Caesar East Salad, 45
Cold Chinese Noodle Salad, 47
Corn Soup, 38
Corned Beef Salad or Sandwich Filling, 53
E-Z Grapefruit Salad, 44
Fried Green Tomatoes Sandwich, 54
Honey of a Spinach Salad, 46
Indoor Grill Veggie Wrap, 58
Oriental Broccoli Slaw, 48
Oriental Chicken Salad, 50
President's Soup, 41
Salt Shakers Salad, 49
Seaburgers, 55
She Crab or Sook Soup, 42
Shrimp or Chicken Poo-Pah's, 56
Soup a L'oignon, 43
Strombolli, 57
Taco Soup, 39
Tortellini and Leek Soup, 40
Walnut & Watercress Salad, 52

Sweet Thang

Arthur Family Christmas Cookies, The, 152
Bacon & Eggs Treat, 144
Black Forest Cheesecake, 137
Brown Sugar Pound Cake, 134
Cheesecake Cookies, 151
Chocolate Fondue, 126
Coffee Ice Cream Dessert, 121
Dates to Remember, 148
E-Z Aloha Brownies with Variations, 139
E-Z Cracker Candy, 145
E-Z Make-Your-Own Ice Cream, 12
0E-Z No Bake Bars for Kids of All Ages, 149
E-Z Peach Deluxe, 127
E-Z Sugar Cinnamon Tortilla Toasties, 147
E-Z White Chocolate Chews, 144
Frozen Peanut Butter Pie, 142
Garden of Eden Baked Apples, 129
Glazed Fresh Blueberry Pie, 141
Grandma Mary's Apple Dumplings, Pennsylvania Style, 131
"Healthy" Oatmeal Cake, 132
Indian Pudding, 123
One Bowl Blonde Brownies, 138
Oranges in Wine, 128
Peach Blossom Ice Cream, 120
Peanut Butter 'n Chocolate Chip Cake, 135
Picnic Fruit Squares, 140
Quick-as-a-Wink Cake, 133
South Carolina Peach Cobbler, 130
Summer's Comin' Strawberry Cheese Cake, 136
To-Die-For Southern Pecan Pie, 143
Toffee Bars, 150
Washday Rainbow Dessert, 122
Winter Hermits, 125
Yule Log Yummies, 146